The Nature of Saving Conversion

(and the way wherein it is wrought)

together with several sermons

by

Solomon Stoddard
of Northampton, Massachussetts

Edited by Rev. Don Kistler

Soli Deo Gloria Publications
. . . for instruction in righteousness . . .

Soli Deo Gloria Publications
P. O. Box 451, Morgan, PA 15064
(412) 221-1901/FAX 221-1902

*

*

ISBN 1-57358-097-X

Contents

The Nature of Saving Conversion

Sermons

Chapter 1

Saving conversion is wrought at once

People are said in Scripture to be converted when they are turned from heathenism to the profession of the truth. So they are said to be turned when there is some notable reformation made among them. But then persons are said to be *savingly* converted when they are turned from the power of Satan unto God, when they have a work of regeneration wrought in them, when they are made holy, and so are justified and made heirs of the kingdom of heaven. And this change is made at once in the soul. It is wrought in the twinkling of an eye.

There is wont, ordinarily, to be a great deal of time spent in way of preparation for this change. In order to this change, there is wont to be a work of contrition and humiliation; and though in primitive times we read of men passing through the work in a very little time, yet ordinarily we find that much time is consumed in the work of preparation. There are many temptations to be overcome, flatteries and discouragements to be removed. Men lose a great deal of time by falling into slumbers, by backwardness to reform some evils, by trying to establish their own righteousness, by fearing that they are not elect, or that God has given them up to hardness of heart, by imagining their hearts to be better than they are, by their unwillingness to own the justice and sovereignty of God. So that commonly several months are spent, and sometimes years, before they get through the work of preparation. Yet conversion itself is wrought at once in the hearing of one passage in a sermon, by the remembering of one Scripture. As it is in the resurrection mentioned in 1 Corinthians 15:52: "In a moment, in the twinkling of an eye, at the last trump; for the trumpet shall sound and the dead shall be raised incorruptible, and we shall be changed," so it is in this first resurrection: "The hour is coming and now is, when the dead shall hear the voice of the Son of God, and they that hear shall live" (John 5:25).

For the clearing of this, consider:

1. That preparatory work is no part of conversion. It is an antecedent to conversion, but no part of conversion. Sometimes under the work of preparation, persons are so exact in their conversation and have such affections and comforts that not only others, but they themselves also think that they are converted. They have very great resemblances of grace; they have many meltings of heart, delight in Sabbaths, zeal against sin as carry a great appearance of a gracious spirit. But all that they attain unto is no part in the work of conversion. They remain still in a natural condition, and their religious affections are but counterfeit graces.

Paul seemed to himself as if he were alive, but afterwards he found himself to be dead. Romans 7:9: "I was alive without the law once, but when the commandment came sin revived and I died." Men under the work of preparation are under the dominion and government of sin; their corruptions are stunned, but not mortified; they are restrained, but not killed. They are like vermin in the winter: stupified, but not dead. And whatever show they make, they are destitute of holiness;

in all their affections there is no love to God; in all their lamentions for sin, there is no godly sorrow. Their religion proceeds only from natural conscience and self love.

These men are afraid of hell, and that makes them walk orderly, resist temptations, and be sorrowful for sin. They hope that God is not so angry as He was, and that makes them forward in duties of religion. They consider the moral evil of many sinful practices, and that begets some kind of loathing in them. They hope in such and such ways to win the favor of God, which makes them forward in duties of religion and charity. They hope sometimes that God has pardoned them, which makes them have strong affections. But all these things are no part of conversion.

It may be said to them as Christ said to the Jews in John 5:42: "You have not the love of God in you." There is not one spark of grace in them. Grace and holiness are quite of another kind. When they have gone through preparation work, conversion remains wholly to be wrought.

2. When the soul has performed one holy action it is converted. One holy action may be performed in the twinkling of an eye. An act of faith in Jesus Christ is done at once. And when the soul has performed one holy action it is converted. If one holy action is performed, there is a principle of grace in the heart; there is a spirit of love, faith, and humility, and such a person is in a state of justification.

There is a great difference between morality and piety on this account. A man may carry temperately, chastely, or justly for a day or two, yet not be a temperate, chaste, or just man. But if he carries holily one day, or one minute, he is a holy man. If he performs one act of faith, he is a believer; if he performs one act of humility, he is a humble man. One act of grace is an evidence that the man's heart is changed, and that he has a principle of grace. Men become morally temperate and chaste by degrees, but they are not made converts by degrees. The least degree of grace makes a man a convert or a saint. Conversion may increase by degrees, men may grow more and more holy by degrees, but conversion is wrought at once. The first act of grace makes a man a convert.

3. Every man is either under the dominion of sin or delivered from the dominion of sin. Those who are not converted are under the dominion of sin, enemies to God, spiritually dead. But those who are converted and delivered from the dominion of sin are subject to God and spiritually alive. Therefore, conversion must be in the twinkling of an eye. If there were any considerable time wherein this work was being done, then at that time the man would neither be under the dominion of sin nor delivered from the dominion of sin. There would be a considerable time wherein he would be neither dead nor alive, and so neither in an estate of condemnation nor justification. But surely the next moment after his being freed from the dominion of sin he is subject to God. The same moment wherein he is delivered from sin, he is a holy man.

Chapter 2

That grace given in saving conversion differs in kind from all that went before

Some have been of the opinion that saving grace and common grace differ only in degrees, that sorrow for sin increases till it becomes saving, and love to God increases till it becomes saving. But, certainly, saving grace differs specifically from all that went before. Gracious actions are of another nature than the religious actions of natural men. The acts of common grace may be very strong and powerful. The affections of the children of Israel were very strong when they sang God's praise (Psalm 106:12). The affections of the Jews to Christ were very strong when they cried, "Hosanna to the Son of David." The affections of the Galatians were strong when, if it had been possible, they would have plucked out their eyes and given them to Paul.

And sometimes the acts of saving grace are very weak. There may be godly sorrow in a low degree; there may be an act of faith with a great mixture of unbelief; there may be true love to God where there is but little love to Him. Grace is low and weak at first, yea, after thirty year's growth it is exceedingly defective. Indeed, true love to God prizes God above all the world, but that does not prove that it is in a great degree. There may be a spirit to prize God before all the world, yet but a small degree of that spirit. Inordinate love to the world is an affecting of that as the chief good; when it is in the lowest degree, it is so—that is the nature of it. So love to God, whether in a greater degree or a less degree, is an affection to God as the chief good. The difference between saving and common grace doesn't lie in the degree, but in the nature of them. This may appear:

1. Because saving grace acts from other motives and for another end than does common grace. The difference in motives and end makes a spiritual difference in actions. If men do not act from gracious motives and for gracious ends, they do not do the thing that God commands. There is no obedience to God in what they do; they don't attend the will of God. When men depend on Christ to save them from the encouragement of their own goodness and merely that they may be delivered from hell, they act quite after another manner than the man does who depends on Christ only from the encouragment of His excellency, and that he may be delivered from sin as well as from damnation. When a man mourns for sin because it exposes him to contempt among men, or wrath from God, or because of the moral evil of it, he does quite another thing from that man who mourns for it because it is a wrong to a God of infinite glory. If his sorrows were in the highest degree that his nature is capable of, it would not be gracious.

2. If the difference between saving grace and common grace lay in the degree, no man could judge that his grace is saving. Men may know that they have saving grace (1 John 3:13; 2 Corinthians 7:10). But if the difference lay in the degree, how would men go about determining that their grace was saving? The man may know that he has a greater degree of confidence, sor-

row, and zeal than he formerly had; he may have reason to think that he goes beyond some other professors in these things, but upon what foundation can he determine that he has them in such a degree as to secure salvation? Where has God revealed what degree is saving and what is not saving? What warrant has any man to judge himself in a safe condition if there are several degrees of grace that are not saving? What rule can any minister lay down to guide men in this matter? Men must be left in a perpetual uncertainty, and remain in the dark about their eternal estate. If a man saw that he believed in Christ, that he repented of his sins, that he aimed at the glory of God, it would be little comfort to him because he could not tell that it was in such a degree as to secure his salvation.

3. The grace that is given in conversion is new. When God converts a man He gives him a new heart and puts a new spirit within him (2 Corinthians 5:17). He is a new creature, not in respect of his soul or the faculties of it, but in respect of the inclinations of it. But if common and saving grace differ only in degree, then his grace is not wholly new for he has had religious joys and sorrows and a zeal a long while. Before he had saving grace, he had the same inclinations and spirit, only now they are heightened and increased. Some degrees are new, but the inclinations themselves are not. So that conversion would not be the giving of a new heart, but only an augmenting of such inclinations as were there before.

4. There is an opposition between saving grace and common grace. If one is opposite to the other, then they differ specifically. Those dispositions that have contrarity one to the other, that are at war with the

other and would destroy one another, are not of the same kind. But truly these are. Common graces are lusts and oppose saving grace. Making his salvation his last end is contrary to making the glory of God his last end. Hating sin because it exposes a man, and not because it wrongs God, is resisting the command of God. Bring everything into subservience to his own ends is opposite to bringing everything into a subservience to God's glory.

The man who has but common grace goes quite in another path than that which God directs him unto. When he goes about to establish his own righteousness, he sets himself against that way of salvation which God prescribes (Romans 10:3). There is an enmity in the ways of such men as have but common grace to the ways that godly men take.

Chapter 3

*Habitual and actual conversion
are wrought together*

Those holy habits and inclinations that God puts
into the hearts of His people are not visible in themselves; men cannot discern them but by their actings.
As men are not able to see their own souls, so they are
not able to see those habits that are in them but by
their actings. They have a power to reflect on the operations of their hearts, and so come to the knowledge of
those habits that are in them; but they cannot see those
habits immediately. Hence no man is able upon his experience to tell the very minute when the habits of
grace were put into him. And generally men have
thought that the habits of grace are put into men before their closing with Christ; and they have been wont
to argue in that manner, that there must be holy principles before holy actions; there must be life before
there are life acts. But there is no necessity of this.

The faculty of acting must be before the action; the
cause must be before the effect; the man must have a
being before he can have any operation. But it does not
follow from hence that there must be a gracious habit
before there is any gracious action. There is no necessity that there is an antecedent habit; it is sufficient if
there is a concomitant habit and inclination. There
was no necessity that Jacob should have a habit of love
to Rachel before he actually loved her; that Michal

9

should have a habit of loving David before she actually loved him. There was no necessity that Adam and Eve should have a habitual inclination to sin before they did sin. So there is no necessity that men should have an inclination to believe in Christ and love God before they actually believe in Christ and love God. It is sufficient that there is a concomitant inclination that way. And thus it is from time to time that, wherever there is an act of faith and love, there is a disposition to act so for the time to come; but there is no necessity in nature that the inclination should be antecedent.

And this supposition of an antecedent gracious inclination before actual conversion is attended with this insuperable difficulty: that a man may have gracious habits and yet be in a state of condemnation, that he may have a sanctified heart, yet be for a long time under the curse, that his heart may be changed and yet abide for a time under the curse, that he may be sanctified yet not justified, for there is no justification till there is actual faith.

When it is said in Scripture that we are justified by faith, the meaning is not that we are justified by a habit of faith, but by actual faith; for that faith is set forth by words signifying action, by believing on Christ, receiving Christ, coming to Christ, opening to Him. It is said of Abraham, "He believed in the Lord and it was counted to him for righteousness" (Genesis 15:6). The condition of justification must be wrought by us; thence it is actual faith that is intended.

A disposition to yield perfect obedience was not the fulfilling of the condition of the covenant of works; if that would have been done, Adam and Eve would have been justified as soon as they were made. So a disposi-

tion to believe is not a fulfilling of the condition of the
covenant of grace, but actual believing is.

Moreover, it is evident that habitual and actual conversion are together because both of them are effected
by the same divine act, which is the discovery of the
truth and glory of the gospel. I am far from thinking
that God is tied up unto this way, or that He cannot give
the habits of grace without such a discovery; but it is evident from the Word of God that He works the habit of
grace and draws forth the act of grace in this way. That
He works this principle and gracious inclination in
this way is plainly taught. 2 Corinthians 3:18: "We all
with open face beholding as in a glass the glory of the
Lord are changed into the same image from glory to
glory, by the Spirit of the Lord."

Changing into the image of God is by giving the
habits of grace unto them. Beholding the glory of God
as in a glass is discerning the glory of God in the
gospel. We are taught the same in 1 Corinthians 4:15: "I
have begotten you through the gospel." In regeneration men receive the habits of grace, the heart is renewed, and the man is made a new man. And this is
wrought through the gospel, by the gospel as understood; for it is in this way and no other that the gospel
has any gracious efficacy on the heart. If a man hears
the gospel twenty years and does not have the spiritual
understanding of it, it will have no gracious effect upon
him. But he discovers what a glorious way of salvation
God has prepared, and that works a great change in his
heart. The same is taught in James 1:18: "Of His own
will begat He us by the word of truth"; that is, by the
gospel, which He calls "the word of truth" by way of excellency, and because the truth of it was questioned by

the Jews and heathens.

And by this discovery God draws forth the exercise of faith at the same time; that discovery makes men immediately to receive the gospel. When men have a spiritual sight of Christ, they will believe on Him. If they withstood the calls before and objected, they will be prevailed on by that sight. John 6:40: "This is the will of Him that sent Me, that every one that seeth the Son and believeth on Him may have everlasting life." And verse 45: "Every man that hath heard and learned of the Father cometh unto Me."

It is also impossible in nature but that men, when they believe in Christ, should have an inclination or disposition to come to Him. Men may do some things out of a kind of compulsion, and do them upon some accident by consideration, and yet hate to do them at the same time. But accepting Christ is always an act of great freedom; when they do it, they do it out of choice. Psalm 110:3: "Thy people shall be willing in the day of Thy power." They do it from conviction of the preciousness of Christ and the benefit of coming to Him. They love to come, and have a disposition to do it for the future.

Chapter 4

Believing in Christ is the first act of conversion

Men who are converted exercise all manner of grace: they perform acts of love, fear, submission, godly sorrow, patience, and humility. But the first act of conversion is to believe in Jesus Christ. There is no other gracious act that goes before faith. In this respect conversion is wrought after the same manner in all who are converted. After the first act of grace there is no certain order in the exercise of graces, but this act of believing in Christ precedes all. Some men do not make a beginning in godliness in loving God, and others in sorrow for sin, and others in patience, and others in humility; but they all begin by receiving Christ as offered in the gospel. False conversions begin some in one way and some in another, but saving conversion always begins with believing in Christ. A man may do a great deal in religion before he believes in Christ, but he has no true love, nor godly sorrow, nor humility before he believes. True holiness takes its rise here. This is the entrance to the strait gate.

There is no sure sign of election before this; therefore we are advised to make our calling and election sure (2 Peter 1:10). This is that which brings men into a state of justification. "He that believeth on Him hath everlasting life" (John 3:36). Whatever went before gave a man no title to life eternal. There is no need for holiness to go before faith. If there were, it would be to encourage men to believe; but there is encouragement enough without that. The grace of God offered in the gospel and the righteousness of Christ are sufficient encouragement, though men never did one good deed; for "God justifieth the ungodly" (Romans 4:5), that is, those who lived an ungodly life till the very minute of their closing with Christ.

Or else, if there was a need of preceding holiness, it would be to incline the heart to come to Christ. But there must be some first act of holiness, and there is no necessity of any preceding holiness to incline men to do the first act of holiness. When God reveals Christ, the heart is then inclined to come to Him. Besides:

1. Sinners, at their first coming to Christ, see nothing in themselves to encourage them to come. When sinners first come to Christ they are weary and heavy laden (Matthew 11:28). They are athirst (Revelation 22:17). They are convinced that their hearts are full of enmity to God, that they are empty of good, that they are wretched and miserable, poor, blind, and naked (Revelation 3:17). Though formerly they thought themselves alive, yet they are convinced that they are dead. They take encouragement from Christ, and the grace and faithfulness of God; but they see no good in themselves to be an encouragement to them.

Afterwards, godly men see something in themselves that is an encouragement to them. They can sometimes say as did David, "I love the Lord" (Psalm 116:1), or as Job, "Thou knowest that I am not wicked" (Job 10:7). And though they depend on Christ and the grace of God alone, yet it is an encouragement to them to see the grace of the Spirit in themselves. But sinners, at their first coming to Christ, see nothing in themselves to be an encouragement to them.

2. Men are sanctified by faith. Acts 26:18: "Sanctified by faith in Me." Acts 15:9: "Purifying their hearts by faith." Their love and repentance are the fruit of faith, and therefore no other holy carriages are antecedent to faith. All who are unbelievers are destitute of other graces. If there are appearances of repentance and love to God's glory, they are but delusions. If other gracious carriages depend on faith, they do not precede faith, for the effect is not before the cause. If faith has no being, it can have no operation. If there were any holiness that went before faith, so that sanctification is not through faith in Christ, then their hearts were purified without faith.

3. The gospel is the means of conversion. It is by the gospel that the hearts of men are made holy. 1 Corinthians 4:15: "I have begotten you through the gospel." The works of creation and common providence teach men to be holy, but do not make men holy. So the law or covenant of works teaches men that they should be holy, but that does not make men holy. It is the gospel that makes men holy.

When Paul was sent to preach the gospel, the design was to turn men from the power of Satan unto God. And if the gospel is the instrument of conversion, men have no holiness till they receive the gospel. So long as the offers of the gospel are rejected or neglected, it can have no sanctifying efficacy on them. It may work some common affections, but it does not change their hearts. If men are not wrought upon by the gospel to give entertainment to Christ, it has no other gracious effect on them. The first gracious effect of the gospel is to make men come to Christ; other gracious effects are consequential to this.

Chapter 5

This act of faith includes all other graces

The act of faith in accepting Jesus Christ is the conversion of the whole soul unto God; for it is virtually all grace. It includes in it something of the spirit of all other graces. There is a distinction in the exercise of several graces. There is a difference between the acts of faith, love, repentance, and humility; yet there is something of the spirit of every grace working in the soul's first closing with Christ.

1. There is a believing of the Word of God. God speaks a great deal in the gospel to encourage sinners to come to Christ. He tells us that He calls us, that Jesus Christ is the Son of God, that He is appointed to be a Prince and a Savior, that He died for our sins, that He has satisfied the justice of God, that He is risen from the dead and sits at the right hand of God, that He will of His free grace pardon all the sins of those who come to Him—and when a man comes to Christ he receives the whole doctrine of the gospel as the true sayings of God. He rejects all carnal reasons, and sets his seal that God is true. He made a profession before, but now he does not stagger at the promise of God through unbelief. He is satisfied that the gospel is no cunningly devised fable, but the very Word of God. 1 Thessalonians 2:13: "Ye received the word not as the word of man, but as it is in truth the word of God, which effectually worketh in you that believe." They do not look upon it as probably, as they did before, but have the assurance of

the truth of it.

2. There is love to God and Christ. When the soul marries Christ, it does it with a spirit of love. It takes God as its portion; it takes its satisfaction in God; it comes to God not for some convenience, but for blessedness; it takes Him as one who is sufficient to make it happy; it despises all the world in comparison to God; it takes a complacency in God and sees the gloriousness and amiableness of God. The love of God appearing in the gospel draws the soul. It loves to depend on Jesus Christ and to put honor upon Him. The way of salvation pleases that soul, and it looks upon Christ as excellent and glorious; it extols Christ. Song of Solomon 5:10: "My beloved is white and ruddy, the chiefest of ten thousands." And verse 16: "He is altogether lovely." The soul's coming to Christ is not a forced thing, but it esteems Him "fairer than the children of men" (Psalm 45:2).

3. There is a spirit of repentance. The converted has stood out a long while against the calls of Christ, but now he repents and changes his mind. Therefore we have that expression in Matthew 9:13: "I am not come to call the righteous, but sinners to repentance." The heart is not affected with grief just at that time only, but dislikes its former course and persists no longer in a way of opposition. The converted man now yields himself to Christ. He says with Isaiah 26:13: "Other lords besides Thee have had dominion over me, but by Thee only will I make mention of Thy name." He now gives himself up to live after another manner than he has done formerly. He has been obstinate a great while, but he stands out no longer. He relinquishes his former way and comes over to Christ. His heart is changed; he

is translated from the kingdom of darkness into the kingdom of Christ.

4. There is humility. All believers are poor in spirit. They are so called in Matthew 5:3. The believer is poor in spirit when he comes under the sense of his unworthiness. When the prodigal returned he said, "I am no more worthy to be called thy son" (Luke 15:19). The man is sensible that nothing but free grace will help him; he depends on the mere mercy of God. Ephesians 2:8: "We are saved by grace." He challenges nothing; he is sensible that he has deserved damnation; he counts that God might fairly destroy him; he does not magnify himself. If he is a man of understanding, if he is wealthy, if he makes a figure in the world, if he has been useful and serviceable to others and to the Church of God, yet he looks upon himself as less than the least of all God's mercies. He takes no encouragement from any excellency in himself; he comes as a poor beggar; he wants pardon and blessedness, but he has nothing to offer God.

The invitation is to such. Isaiah 55:1: "Ho, everyone that thirsteth, come ye to the waters, and he that hath no money, come ye, buy and eat; yea, come buy wine and milk without money and without prices." And when a man comes to Christ, he comes empty, willing to be beholding to Christ for all. He desires salvation, and is willing that God and Christ should have the glory of it. He comes for free grace; his language is as Psalm 130:7: "With the Lord there is mercy, and with Him is plenteous redemption."

5. There is self-denial. Under the work of humiliation he was forced out of himself. He saw his own righteousness was as filthy rags; he saw there was nothing

in it to depend upon; he saw his best works were just ground of condemnation. But when he sees the preciousness of Christ's righteousness, that mortifies a self-righteous spirit. He sees there is no comparison between them; he sees his own righteousness is but dross compared with that gold tried in the fire. He is willing for the sake of Christ's righteousness to part with his own. Philippians 3:7: "What things were gain to me, those I counted loss for Christ."

Formerly, when he was invited to come to Christ, he had many reasonings in his own heart against that way; but now he is satisfied in the wisdom of God and denies his own wisdom. He will not listen to any cavils, but says of Christ that He is the power of God and the wisdom of God (2 Corinthians 1:24), and that in Him are hidden all the treasures of wisdom and knowledge. So he denies his own power and rests upon the power of Christ to deliver him from temptation, and to keep him from sin and preserve him to salvation.

6. There is a spirit of thankfulness. When a man sees Christ offered to him, and pardon and salvation upon His account, he looks upon it as an unspeakable mercy and receives it as a great gift of grace. He was wont formerly to slight the offer and cast contempt upon it, to neglect to receive it; but now he looks upon it as a wonderful offer. He has honorable thoughts of the grace of God; his heart is affected with God's mercy and comes gladly to Christ. He counts the gospel good news and is sensible that God therein shows great kindness. He counts it a great opportunity. He looks upon himself as greatly beholden to God. His heart is ready to leap for joy. He accepts the invitation and blesses the name of God. He says that "it is a faithful

saying and worthy of all acceptation, that Christ Jesus came into the world to save sinners" (1 Timothy 1:15).

7. There is a spirit of universal obedience. When God opens the eyes to see the call of the gospel, men are sensible that it is the will of God that they should come to Christ. That is God's great command (1 John 3:23), and in obedience to God they come. They dare not rebel against God's call. Besides, there is a spirit of obedience in receiving Christ as their King. They accept Christ as He is offered. God has made Christ the King of His Church, and offers Him as such; and when a man accepts Him he takes Him as his Lord as well as his Savior. He knows that Christ requires universal holiness, religion, truth, justice, chastity, temperance, and charity, and he accepts Christ as his Lord. He is willing to be subject to His laws and government. Their voice is, "The Lord is our Judge, the Lord is our Law-giver, and He will save us" (Isaiah 33:22).

These men receive Christ in all His offices. They come with a spirit of obedience. Besides, when they come to Christ, they come to Him to enable them to lead holy lives; they depend on Him for strength to overcome their temptations that He may be made sanctification unto them (1 Corinthians 1:30). They depend upon His help that they may live holy lives. Galatians 2:20: "I live by faith in the Son of God."

Chapter 6

The infusion of grace mortifies corruption

By putting grace into the heart, God destroys the power of sin. Natural men are not able to mortify their own corruptions. Whatever improvement they make of their natural abilities and outward opportunities, they will fall short of mortifying their corruptions. They may do several things in order to mortify their sins, but they cannot effect it. They may restrain themselves greatly from the acts of sin, but chopping down the tree does not kill the root. If they do not make provision for the flesh, yet they cannot starve it. If they bewail their sins and cry out against them, and even call themselves madmen, that will not do it. Pharaoh bewailed his sin (Exodus 9:27), and Judas his (Matthew 27:3), yet both of them were far from mortification. Yea, if they study the danger and evil of their sins, that will not serve the turn.

Such men may consider that if their sins don't die their souls must die, according to Romans 8:13: "If ye live after the flesh ye shall die, but if ye through the Spirit do mortify the deeds of the flesh, ye shall live." They may think that sin is dishonorable and unprofitable, that there is ingratitude, injustice, and impudence in it. If we consider such things a thousand times over, that will not mortify our corruptions; it is God who does it, and the way wherein He does it is by infusing a principle of grace into the heart. The infusion of grace and the mortification of corruption are at the same time, instant. Mortification of corruption doesn't follow after the infusion of grace, but is contemporary with it. 2 Corinthians 5:17: "Old things are passed away, and all things are made new."

These two works are done by the same operation. God does not put forth two operations, one to make men gracious and the other to kill their corruptions; but the same divine act has these two effects: to give new inclinations and destroy the old. God restrains the corruptions of men before He puts grace into them, and He takes away much of those evil habits that men had contracted by a course of sin. He does that by terrifying the conscience, giving some common encouragements, and by human restraints and education; but it is by giving grace to the soul that corruption is mortified. Corruption is not mortified before the infusion of grace, neither is the infusion of grace before mortification, but they are wrought at once by the same act.

ARGUMENT 1. The same light that works gracious inclinations destroys sin. The way wherein God communicates grace is by teaching men how glorious He is. He lets in gospel light and so works gracious inclinations. Men see the reason why they should love God, trust in Christ, and be humble, and this inclines the heart that way. God deals with men as with rational creatures: He reveals to them the reason and foundation of holy carriages, and so disposes the heart to them. 2 Corinthians 3:18: "We all beholding as in a glass the glory of the Lord are changed into the same image." He makes them know Himself, and so makes them sincere. Psalm 36:10: "Stretch forth Thy lovingkindness to them that know Thee, and Thy righteousness to the upright in heart." He teaches them, and so they come to Christ. John 6:45: "Every one that hath heard and learned of the Father cometh unto Me."

And it is the same way that He mortifies their corruption. This light weans them from the world; it kills the pride of their hearts. This light makes them hate the ways of sin. At the same time that they see reason to exalt God, they see the evil of pride. When they see reason to love God, they see that there is no reason to dote on the world. Acts 26:18: "To turn them from darkness to light, and from the power of Satan to God."

ARGUMENT 2. Natural corruption is nothing else but the privation of holiness. Contracted habits have something positive in them, but natural corruption is only the privation of holiness. When man lost the image of God, there was nothing positive put into him. The condition of man by nature is that he is destitute of love, faith, and humility; and thence he runs into evil, is disposed to love the world, and set himself above God. This shows that the very giving of grace mortifies corruption. When the habit is given, the privation is expelled. When light comes into the eye, the darkness is gone; when sight is given to men, blindness is taken away. When life came to Lazarus, he was delivered from death; when love to God is put into the soul, inordinate self-love is mortified. When faith is wrought in the heart, unbelief is mortified; when men are made humble, their pride is mortified; when God conveys spiritual life to men without any more to do, they are delivered from spiritual death. Romans 8:2: "The law of the spirit of life in Christ Jesus has made us free from the law of sin and death."

ARGUMENT 3. Holiness implies in it a hatred to

sin. Where sin is hated, it is mortified. This was Paul's spirit: "What I hate, that I do" (Romans 7:15). When sin is hated, then the strength of it is abated. The strength of sin lies in men's love to sin. Wherever sin is hated as the greatest evil, it is mortified. As it loses the love of men, so it loses its strength. It was a sign of David's mortification that he hated vain thoughts (Psalm 119:113). And wherever there is holiness there is a hatred of sin. If the heart of a man is inclined to believe, he hates unbelief. Unbelief is contrary to that inclination; so if a man has an inclination to love God as his chief good, he will hate the workings of pride and worldliness, the setting up of any other thing above God.

Sinful inclinations are enemies to holiness and holy inclinations are enemies to sin. They have a tendency to destroy one another. Galatians 5:17: "The flesh lusteth against the Spirit, and the Spirit against the flesh, and these are contrary the one to the other." There is a warfare between grace and corruption; they seek the destruction of one another.

ARGUMENT 4. The more degrees of grace men get, the more sin is mortified. The more men put on the new man, the more they put off the old man. Holiness and mortification hold an exact proportion one to the other. As one scale rises, the other falls. As water comes into the vessel, the air is expelled. The more light is in the air, the less darkness. 2 Samuel 3:1: "David waxed stronger and stronger, as the house of Saul waxed weaker and weaker."

As grace flourishes, so sin dies. Whenever there is any addition to grace, there is a proportionate subtraction from corruption. The more humility, the less pride. Those who are very humble are not very proud. They who have a great deal of faith have but little unbelief. And when grace shall be perfected, no sin shall remain. The perfection of grace expels all sin. Where there is perfect light there is no darkness. 1 John 1:5: "God is light, and in Him is no darkness at all." Where there is perfect beauty there is no blemish. Ephesians 5:27: "Not having spot or wrinkle, or any such thing; but that it should be holy without blemish."

Chapter 7

Conversion is wrought by light

God is the Author of conversion. Men must be born of the Spirit. Whatever means are used will be ineffectual if there is not the operation of the Spirit. James 1:18: "Of His own will begat He us." Such as are converted are born of God (John 1:13). And the way wherein He does it is by letting spiritual light into the soul, by irradiating the mind, letting in beams of light into the heart. In that way God increases grace, and in that way He gives grace at first. While men remain in darkness they remain in the kingdom of darkness, but by enlightening the mind He changes the heart. It is by inward discoveries of the glory of God that He sanctifies the heart.

In this way the gospel becomes a rod of strength. Psalm 110:2: "The Lord shall send forth the rod of Thy strength out of Zion." Spiritual light prevails immediately upon the heart. Men who have refused a long while refuse no longer after God lets in this light. Acts 26:18: "To open their eyes, to turn from darkness to light, and from the power of Satan unto God." 2 Corinthians 3:18: "We all with open face beholding in a glass the glory of the Lord, are changed into the same image, from glory to glory, as by the Spirit of the Lord." All who are ignorant of God remain unconverted; all who know God are converted.

ARGUMENT 1. Man's being capable of knowing God makes him capable of being holy. If man did not have a reasonable soul capable of knowing God he could not be capable of being holy. The inferior creatures, though they have some knowledge and resemblances of reason, yet are incapable of the knowledge of God and, accordingly, incapable of holiness, and accordingly are not under the direction of the moral law. But if God makes man capable of knowing Him, He thereby makes him capable of holiness. The reason is because if he actually knows God he will be holy. The knowledge of God and holiness go together. Psalm 36:10: "Stretch forth Thy lovingkindness to them that know Thee, and Thy righteousness to the upright in heart."

God is so glorious that if He is known the heart will be drawn to Him. Psalm 30:7: "Because of the excellency of Thy loving kindness, the children of men put their trust in the shadow of Thy wings." The excellency of God draws the heart irresistibly to Him when it is known. The knowledge of God is inseparable from holiness. All who know Him are holy. The very capacity to know God makes men capable of being holy, of loving Him and trusting in Him. The angelic nature is capable of knowing God, and so is capable of holiness; and so is the human nature. When men are renewed in the image of God, they are renewed in knowledge. Colossians 3:10: "And have put on the new man, which is renewed in knowledge, after the image of Him that created him."

ARGUMENT 2. Until men know God, no terror, punishment, or persuasion will make them holy. Many men have strong persuasions set before them to induce them to be holy. The equity of it, the profit, the pleasure, and the honor of it are amply demonstrated—

such arguments as are wont mightily to prevail in other cases, yet the men are not gained; they make their hearts as adamants, and they will not be gained until they have the knowledge of God.

If the persuasions beget some desires, if they beget some resolutions, if they prevail on men to make some attempts, yet they do not make men holy. Men must be taught of God, else they will not be holy. John 6:45: "Every man that hath heard and learned of the Father cometh unto Me."

Terrors of conscience will not make men holy. Men cannot be frightened into the love of God. Men may be sacred into reformation, but not into conversion. Trembling may take hold of hypocrites, yet they remain hypocrites. Cain's terrors did not make him holy. Judas' terrors did not make him holy. Fear will make men hypocrites, but not saints. Psalm 78:34: "When He slew them, then they sought Him," but, verse 36, "They flattered Him with their mouth, and lied unto Him with their tongue." The fear of hell will not make men hate sin more than hell. Punishments will not make men holy. Hell fire will not purge away men's dross. One glimpse of the glory of God will do more than all the punishments in the world to make men holy. Song of Solomon 1:4: "Draw me and I will run after thee."

ARGUMENT 3. The perfect knowledge of God is accompanied with perfect holiness. Holiness always holds a proportion to men's knowledge of the glory of God. They who have not the knowledge of the glory of God have not one spark of holiness; if they pretend to it, yet they are utterly destitute of it. Men may set up altars to the unknown god, but they never love an unknown god. And when there is the beginning of the knowledge of God, there is the beginning of holiness; and as the knowledge increases, so holiness increases. They keep pace with each other; they are in exact proportion to one another. Every beam of light has heat in it. 2 Peter 1:2: "Grace and peace be multiplied to you through the knowledge of God, and of our Savior, Jesus Christ." And when the knowledge of God is perfect, holiness will be perfect. We can never comprehend God, nor search out the Almighty to perfection; yet the grace of knowledge may be perfect. And when men enjoy the light of glory, they will be as holy as they desire to be. Light and life will be perfected together. Heaven is a place of perfect light and perfect holiness. Psalm 17:5: "I shall behold His face in righteousness, I shall be satisfied with Thy likeness." 1 John 3:2: "We shall be like Him, for we shall see Him as He is."

ARGUMENT 4. When men see the glory of God, they would be acting against their nature if they should not be holy. Every creature will act its nature, and so will man. When men know things to be true, they will assent to them. When men see God, they know His testimony to be true. When men know the excellency of God, they must choose Him. The glory of God is such that it captivates the heart; where it is seen it has a magnetic power; it irresistably conquers the will. There is a necessity of loving God when He is seen. If men should not, they would act against their nature. There is no power in the will to resist holiness when the glory of God is seen. It is impossible in nature that men should know God and not be holy. The will always follows the last dictates of the understanding. The understanding is the guide of the will; the will always follows its direction. Men would offer violence to their nature if they should do otherwise. The excellency of God is a sufficient reason for men's loving and serving Him. Because God has such excellency, it is man's duty to love and serve Him; and it is their happiness to love and serve Him. And when they know the excellency of God it will be their practice. The gloriousness of God has a commanding power on the heart.

Chapter 8

*Men are capable of receiving light from the Spirit
of God before they have a habitual change
in their understanding*

Man, in his natural estate, is represented in Scripture as utterly depraved, dead in trespasses and sins. He is blind and in darkness. It may be thought that he is incapable of seeing the gloriousness of God until there is first a habitual change in his understanding; but if we examine the Word of God we may find plain intimations that this light precedes the habitual change. John 5:25: "The time is coming, and now is, when the dead shall hear the voice of the Son of God; and they that hear shall live." Hearing the voice of Christ is antecedent to their living. It is in that way that life enters upon them. 2 Corinthians 3:18: "We all with open face beholding as in a glass the glory of the Lord are changed into the same image."

Before they are changed into God's image, they behold His glory. This makes it evident that men are capable of beholding the glory of the Lord before the habitual change. God reveals His glory, and that inclines a man to assent, and draws forth an actual assent. This may be further considered by these arguments:

ARGUMENT 1. Man, in his corrupted state, has his natural faculty of understanding. He has the faculty of understanding in his corrupted state and in his renewed state. A godly man does not have two faculties of understanding—one whereby he knows God and another whereby he knows other things—but by the faculty of understanding he knows God and Christ, the truth of promises, and likewise rules of art, the motions of the sun and moon, and the natural causes.

Where there is a natural understanding, endued with literal knowledge and assisted by the Spirit of God, there is a power to know God. In that case, there is nothing wanting in order to the spiritual knowledge of God. Men need no other faculty in order to spiritual knowledge, provided it is duly enlightened. To imagine that there needs to be any other power is to fancy the need of another faculty, or a faculty in a faculty, in order to the knowledge of God—as if we understood the creature by one faculty and God by another. A faculty of understanding instructed and assisted by the Spirit must enable men to know God.

ARGUMENT 2. A habitual change in the understanding does not give men a power to know God. It must be acknowledged that there is such a thing as a habitual change in the understanding. Godly men have a sanctified mind; they have a principle put into them that leads them to judge aright concerning God and Christ, and a principle of faith to receive the testimony of God. But habits do not give men a power to know. We must carefully distinguish between a faculty or power and a habit. A habit is only an inclination to do a thing; a habit fits a man to do a thing with more facility and dexterity. Habits are not faculties; they do not enable men to do what they could not do before, they merely dispose and incline the heart that way. A natural man has a prevailing inclination to judge wrongly concerning God and an opposition to believe rightly concerning God. His mind is averse to the reception of those doctrines that the Scripture teaches concerning God; but yet he has the faculty or power to judge aright when he is assisted. And the godly man, having received habitual light, has an inclination to judge aright of God and spiritual things.

ARGUMENT 3. This actual light which men receive from the Spirit of God begets habitual light. It is in this case as in many others: a man who has had experience of the sweetness of honey is inclined thereby to judge so from time to time. He has had that experience of the saltiness of the sea and is inclined to judge it so. And he who has understood the gloriousness of God is prepared and disposed thereby to judge so from time to time. This discovery leaves such a sense and impression on the heart as inclines it forever to judge so concerning God. They never forget what they have seen, and so are inclined to judge after the like manner. And the more frequently they have eminent discoveries of God and Christ, the more strongly they are inclined to judge so, and to reject the contrary temptations. Repeated discoveries strengthen the habit and dispose them with more readiness to judge so. The inclination to judge aright of God is a rational inclination, flowing from a conviction of the gloriousness of God.

Chapter 9

*The first thing this light discovers is
the gloriousness of God*

Many men who have had experience of this spiritual light are able to give a very poor account of how it works at first in their heart. The understanding is so quick in its operations that the steps of these discoveries that are made to the soul do not fall under their observation. They may be able to give some account of what they saw, that they saw such and such encouragement to come to Christ, but they do not know how they came to be convinced of it. But we have abundant cause to conclude that the first discovery that is made is of the gloriousness of God. The knowledge of God is the foundation of all religion. Psalm 36:10: "Stretch forth Thy hand in lovingkindness to them that know Thee, and Thy righteousness to the upright in heart." John 17:3: "This is eternal life, that they may know Thee, the only true God, and Jesus Christ whom Thou hast sent." Two things will make this evident:

ARGUMENT 1. The spiritual knowledge of God does not depend upon the spiritual knowledge of other things. There does not need to be any antecedent discoveries in order to the spiritual knowledge of God. When God opens the eyes of men and gives spiritual understanding to them, there are two ways wherein they may see the glory of God:

1. By reasoning from the works of creation and com-

mon providence. There is a great discovery of the glory of God in making the world. Psalm 19:1: "The heavens declare the glory of God and the firmament showeth His handiwork." Isaiah 6:3: "The whole earth is full of His glory." And when they behold the work of God they may readily see, if their eyes are opened, that these things were made by a God of infinite power, wisdom, and goodness. There is a self-evidencing light in these works of God, showing that they are the effects of a God of infinite glory.

The world is a glass, reflecting the glory of God; and when men's eyes are opened they may plainly see it. So in other great works of God: the great deluge, the burning of Sodom, the delivery of Israel out of Egypt, maintaining them in the wilderness. God often puts us in mind that He has created the heavens and laid the foundations of the earth. That is an abundant manifestation to those who understand that He is a glorious God, worthy to be believed, loved, and obeyed. When men's eyes are opened, they see the force of the argument; they are at once satisfied about the glorious properties of God. Reason enlightened by the Spirit of God teaches men convincingly what God is.

2. By reasoning from the Word of God. The Word of God has a self-evidencing light in it; it shows that it proceeds from a God of infinite glory. The holiness of the law and the wisdom and grace that appear in the gospel are in themselves very evidential of God's glory. And though multitudes of men who read and hear the Word are not convinced of the divine authority of it, yet, when God lets in beams of spiritual light, they receive it as the Word of God; they are convinced that it proceeds from a God of infinite glory. When God

shines into the heart, they see the glory of God in the face of Jesus Christ (2 Corinthians 4:6). With an open face, they behold as in a glass the glory of the Lord (2 Corinthians 4:18). They say, "Such things would never have entered into the heart of man if God had not revealed them" (1 Corinthians 2:9).

ARGUMENT 2. The spiritual knowledge of other things depends on the spiritual knowledge of God. The knowledge of particular revealed truths depends on the knowledge of God. Until people know God, they can have no faith; faith depends upon the knowledge of God. Until they know God, they do not see a foundation for faith, nor know anything that is to be known only by faith. Until men know God, they cannot know the saving benefit of the blood of Christ, the divinity of Christ, the promises, or the happiness of heaven; for all faith depends upon our assurance of the faithfulness of God.

But once we are convinced of the faithfulness of God, we are prepared to believe whatever God has revealed. If God reveals things that are beyond natural reason to comprehend, such as the doctrine of the Trinity or the Incarnation of the Son of God, such men will believe it; if God reveals things that are very contrary to carnal reason, as that God is angry with carnal men though they live in great prosperity, and that He lights in godly men and will save them, though they are low and in great affliction; if He promises pardon to those who have been very sinful if they accept the offers of the gospel, such men will believe it—the consideration of the faithfulness of God will overcome all objections.

If men were at never so much loss about the truth of

them before, and rejected them as false, or suspended their belief, looking on them as uncertain; yet as soon as ever they understood the faithfulness of God, the darkness of their minds would be removed. That man would see a foundation for faith, and so these things which were mysteries to him before are now heartily acknowledged. Hebrews 11:7: "Faith is the evidence of things not seen."

Chapter 10

The soul, being convinced of the gloriousness of God, sees encouragement to accept Christ

Multitudes who are called to come upon one occasion or the another excuse themselves. Yea, men who are in great distress for the want of forgiveness reject the offer. They would fain be pardoned, and pray to God to accept them upon Christ's account; but they dare not accept the offer of mercy. They have all manner of persuasions, but remain unpersuadable; they resolve to do it, they may attempt it, but do not effect it. It seems a dangerous thing and a method to cast away their own souls. They think God would be very angry with them for obtruding themselves upon Him. It seems to them a desperate adventure. But when they are convinced of the gloriousness of God, they see encouragements enough to come to Christ.

They see three things especially that are encouragements to them:

1. The free grace of God. They were wont to discourage themselves because of their unworthiness; it seemed to them as if the heart of God was turned against them, and they labored that they might get something to incline the heart of God towards them, something that might appease His anger and attract His love. But when they have the knowledge of God, they are satisfied in the freeness of His grace; they see that there is enough in His own heart to move Him,

that there is an infinite ocean of grace there, that His thoughs are not as our thoughts, that there is a height, a depth, a length, and a breadth in the love of God that passes knowledge, and that He can pity His greatest enemies and love those who have nothing to commend them.

They say He is God and not man. His mercy does not depend on any excellency in them. His grace is sovereign grace, and He has mercy on whom He will have mercy. Though it is a great thing to be pardoned and saved, yet it is not too much for Him to do. There is no need of anything to move His heart. He can do it because it pleases Him. They were wont formerly to limit the mercy of God and to think it would have been sufficient if they had not been such great sinners, or if they were more broken for their sins. But now they are convinced that if they were worse than they are the mercy of God is sufficient for them; that there is an infiniteness in the grace of God. And after they have reckoned up many things that grace can do, there is infinitely more than they can think of. No badness discourages them, no want of goodness discourages them. There is no more limiting the grace of God than there is the power of God. There is mercy enough to set against their unworthiness. Psalm 36:7: "How excellent is Thy lovingkindness, O God, therefore the children of men put their trust under the shadow of Thy wings."

2. The preciousness and sufficiency of Christ's righteousness. The threatenings of the law were a terror to them, like a burning sword. They saw justice binding them over to condemnation. They thought that every jot and tittle of the law must be fulfilled, as in Matthew 5:18; that the law cannot be abrogated nor moderated;

that all the challenges of it must be answered. And
when they heard of the satisfaction of Christ, that did
not satisfy their consciences. They were told that Christ
Jesus was the Son of God, that God had appointed Him
to be a mediator, that His sacrifice was acceptable to
God. And they looked upon those things very probably,
but were not certain of them. But when they see God
and believe His Word, Christ is precious to them
(2 Peter 2:7).

They look on Him just according to the report of
the gospel. They say, as did Peter in Matthew 16, He is
"the Christ, the Son of the living God." They are sensible that He has redeemed us from the curse, having
born the curse for us; that He has made reconciliation
for iniquity, made an end of sin, and brought in an everlasting righteousness; that in the Lord Jesus we have
righteousness and strength. They are satisifed that He
has made a new and living way to the holy place.

They see now that the guilt of sin was translated to
Christ, that the law has been executed on Him, that His
blood has quenched the fire of God's wrath, that an
atonement is made and God is reconciled, that Christ
is at the right hand of God, exalted to be a Prince and a
Savior, that it is a safe thing to appear before God in
His righteousness; there is no need of any addition to
it. They say there are unsearchable riches in Christ.
Before, they did not know but that the doctrine concerning Christ was a delusion, a cunningly devised fable; but now they are sure it is otherwise. John 6:69: "We
believe and are sure that Thou art that Christ, the Son
of the living God." John 17:8: "They have known surely
that I came from Thee, and they believed that Thou did
send Me."

3. The faithfulness of the offers of the gospel. God in the gospel makes many gracious promises. He promises that such as come to Jesus Christ He will in no wise cast out (John 6:37); that those who believe in Christ shall not perish, but shall have everlasting life (John 3:16); that all who believe in Christ shall have remission of sins (Acts 10:43). And this light gives assurance of the truth of the promises. Before this light was given they seemed incredible. Sometimes they doubted them because of the greatness of them, sometimes because God was angry with them, sometimes because there were but few who were saved. But when this light comes into the soul, they see the certainty of these promises; they come with a divine authority upon the heart. 1 Thessalonians 2:13: "Ye received the word, not as the word of man, but as it was indeed the word of God."

The faithfulness of God convinces them that the promise is sure. They do not build their persuasions upon the opinions of men, but upon the Word of God. Many men dispute with a great deal of confidence for the principles of religion against papists and Socinians, but it is upon the supposition that the Scripture is the Word of God, and that they take for granted, but do not know it. But when this spiritual light is let into them, they are assured of the divine authority of the Scriptures. They are assured it is the Word of God, and know that God is faithful. They say with David in Psalm 12:6: "The words of the Lord are pure words, as silver tried in a furnace of earth, purified seven times."

Chapter 11

No man is able to give a full account of all that he saw when this light first shone in his heart

There is a great deal of difference in this light as to the clearness of it; all who have this spiritual light do not see things with the same clearness. The discoveries are more dim in some than in others. There are degrees of natural light, so of the light of reason, so of spiritual light. This light is sometimes called wisdom. Sometimes, because of the clearness of it, it is called revelation. Ephesians 1:17: "That God would give unto you the spirit of wisdom and revelation in the knowledge of Him."

But whether the sight is clear or more obscure, they all see the truth of the gospel, that Christ is a sufficient foundation for them to build upon, and that it is safe to cast themselves upon Him; that Christ is precious, and that the gospel is of divine authority. But no man is able to give an exact account of all that he will see at that time. The thing was done in the twinkling of an eye, and though men never forget it yet they cannot call to mind all that they were convinced of; no, not if they were to give an account the next hour. Men do not have at that time the actual understanding of all gospel principles. Indeed, they saw that the way of salvation that they had been instructed in for many years was true, but they do not have the actual understanding of it at the very time. Yet they saw and actually understood at the time a great deal more than they can remember. This may appear by these things:

1. From the shortness of the time wherein this discovery is made. There is but very little time between the opening of the eyes and the heart's closing with Christ; and the discovery is wont to last but a little time. So it is impossible that he should have a distinct remembrance of everything that he saw. The spouse gives a very particular description of Christ in figurative expressions (Song of Solomon 5, from verse 16 to the end). And so godly men are able to do from what they find in the Word of God; but they can remember but a little account of what they saw at that time.

If a man casts up his eyes to heaven, he sees a multitude of stars, but is not able to give a particular account of what he saw of the several stars and constellations. So if a man should cast his eye upon a beautiful person, he is much affected with their beauty, but he can't give a particular account of all their features, the comeliness of their forehead, eyes, cheeks, or lips, or give a description of them. If a man should cast his eye upon a garden where there is a variety of flowers, he may be much affected with it yet not be able to tell particularly what sorts of flowers he saw. Or, if he should cast his eye upon a curious piece of embroidery, he may perceive immediately that there is much curiosity in it, but he cannot give an account of all the colors and remembrances that he cast his eye upon.

Thus it is when men's eyes are opened. They see the way of salvation to be a glorious way, but they cannot tell particularly all they saw. They had but a transient sight and could not take such distinct notice of things as to lay them up in their memory.

2. There is need of the actual knowledge of many gospel truths in order to the first closing with Christ. They heard of those things often before, but they understood nothing in a right manner before—but they must understand them in order to close with Christ. They need to understand something of the greatness of that salvation that is offered. Men will not accept the offer unless they judge it worthy to be accepted. They need to understand that the offer is made to them; the making of such an offer to others is no warrant to them to accept thereof. They need to understand that their sins may be pardoned, that the law does not render them incapable of pardon. They need to understand that it is God Himself who makes the offer in the gospel. Nothing less than that can be an encouragement to accept.

Men need to understand that God has mercy enough to pardon all their sins, though they have no worthiness. If they do not understand this, they will not dare to accept the offer. They need to understand the faithfulness of God or else they can see no safety in coming to Christ. They need to understand the saving virtue of the blood of Christ, that it is acceptable to God and sufficient to purge away sin. They need to understand that Christ Jesus is the Son of God, that they may be satisfied in the divine virtue of His blood. They need to understand that God made Him a Mediator and wounded Him for our transgressions. They need to understand the sufficiency of Christ to sanctify them and make them persevere, and God's ability to fulfill His promises. And there is no godly man who can recover the remembrance of it, that at that time he saw all these things.

3. Some can remember more than others, but none can call to mind all that he saw at that time; because at that time men's thoughts are so fixed upon one or two particular things that they are hindered thereby from remembering some other things. Experience shows that some men at their first conversion have their thoughts more fixed on the consideration of the free mercy of God. They see a depth of compassion in the heart of God, that He has no need of any external motive to draw His heart, that He can overlook all manner of provocations, and that He has mercy on whom He will, and compassion on whom He will have compassion (Romans 9:15).

Some men at the time had their thoughts more taken up about the sacrifice of Christ, how He has borne the curse, bought us with a price, made His soul an offering for sin, and fully satisfied the justice of God. And some others have their thoughts at that time more fixed upon the faithfulness of God, that His words are pure words, that He is not a man that He should lie, nor the Son of Man that He should repent, that His Word is a sure foundation to build upon.

It is frequently so afterwards. They are led into it sometime by the consideration of some Scripture that comes to mind at that time; sometimes by having special temptations just before, as if God could not find in His heart to pardon such as they, as if Christ's blood would not answer for their sins. And the thoughts being fixed on one encouragement makes others less observed.

If a man takes particular notice of one argument in a discourse, he can give the less account of the rest. If a man takes special notice of what concerns himself in a discourse, he will not take such particular notice of what concerns others. If there is a great show, one person takes more notice of one particular, another of another, and they are not able to give a good account of the other things that they saw.

Chapter 12

This spiritual light reveals those things that men were convinced of before under the work of preparation, and that in a better manner than they saw them before

Before God converts men, it is His manner to prepare them for it by a common work of His Spirit, which is called "preparatory." This makes men sensibly seek after reconciliation. Men are called upon to seek first the kingdom of God and His righteousness, to labor not for the meat that perishes, but for that meat that endures unto eternal life. And men are blamed for slightly seeking (Luke 13:24). Many seek and are not able to enter. And the happiness of some was that their hearts were mightily set in seeking the kingdom of God (Matthew 11:13).

Men are laboring, some a long while, for peace with God before they are converted. Convinced of the vanity of the world and of the necessity of the favor of God and eternal life, convinced also of the insufficiency of their own righteousness, they relinquish those; but when God lets in spiritual light to convert men, it reveals the same that they saw under the work of preparation, and in a better manner than they saw before.

When God gives spiritual light and reveals His grace and the glory of Christ to the soul, that reveals those things that they saw under the works of preparation.

It will reveal the terribleness of damnation. One thing that

47

sinners are sensible of under the work of preparation is that the wrath of God is terrible. And they are wont to cry out as the jailer, "What must I do to be saved?" (Acts 16:30). Or as David in Psalm 48:3: "There is no soundness in my flesh because of Thine anger, nor any rest in my bones because of my sin." They see that they have exposed themselves to the heavy wrath of God and are liable to damnation, which is intolerable. Isaiah 33:14: "Who can dwell with devouring fire, who can dwell with everlasting burnings?" And the sense of this is wont to fill them with terror.

They are afraid of dying quickly, and are urged in spirit to cry out to God and beg pardon of their sins. This stirs them up carefully to reform their lives, to leave off all sinful practices, and to resist temptations. This makes them sensible of the vanity of the world.

And when gospel light is let into men, they will see the terribleness of the wrath of God for sin. If they did not see that, they would not see the necessity of coming to Christ for salvation; but when they see the truth of the gospel, they will be convinced of that, for then they will see the faithfulness of God and the truth of the threatenings of the law. Then they will believe the greatness of Christ's sufferings, and thereby see the terrible wrath of God for sin. Luke 23:31: "If these things be done in the green tree, what shall be done in the dry?" In the sorrows of Christ they will discern how intolerable the wrath of God is, and what need there is of deliverance from it.

It will reveal the vanity and insufficiency of men's own righteousness. Under the work of preparation they are, by degrees, led into the understanding of their own unworthiness, that they can do nothing to pacify the wrath or merit the favor of God. When sinners are in distress of conscience, they are wont to labor to lay some bonds on the justice, faithfulness, or mercy of God; and in length of time God is wont to show them that their righteousness does not answer the law, satisfies for no sin, cannot draw the heart of God to them; that by their best works they are meriting condemnation; that their hearts are full of enmity to God; that they have no power to do any good; that they have nothing of their own to depend upon, but stand in need of the grace and the righteousness of Christ. And when the gospel light is let into them, it teaches them the emptiness of their own works.

When men see the excellency of Christ's righteousness, they see it as a vain thing for them to think to pacify God themselves. They shall never be able to get anything of their own that is comparable to the righteousness of Christ. That alone will serve their turn, and they have no need of any other. Philippians 3:7: "What things were gain to me, those I counted loss for Christ." When men see their own hearts under the work of humiliation, they see the vanity of their own righteousness; but when they see the righteousness of Christ, they see further into the vanity of it and prefer Christ's righteousness, and count their own as dung in comparison with Christ's. Philippians 3:8: "And count them but dung that I may win Christ."

They are convinced of these things after a better manner than they were under the work of preparation. Under the work of preparation men are convinced of them by the illumination of natural conscience. They see that there is a great danger of damnation, that damnation is intolerable, and that the world is vain. They see that their own righteousness cannot draw the heart of God, and that it is just with God to destroy them.

Some things they are convinced of by experience, such as that they are blind and under the dominion of their sins; that they are dead in trespasses and sins. But when spiritual light is let into them, they know these things after a better manner. Then they see these by faith; they believe the testimony of God in His Word, and this has a better effect upon the heart. He sees so much of the world that he hates a worldly spirit; he sees the vanity of a worldly spirit so that it is mortified ever after. He sees the vanity of his own righteousness and hates a self-righteous spirit.

Chapter 13

The way considered wherein God, by this spiritual light, converts men or makes them holy

When man is in his corrupt state, the essence of the soul remains entire, and that natural disposition remains in the will to follow the last dictates of the understanding. So that when God makes this change in the understanding, there is always a proportionate change made in the will. When God makes an understanding He makes a will, and when He renews the understanding He renews the will. They are not two things, but one and the same soul, diversely denominated according to two several ways of working which are inseparably conjoined. When the soul has this spiritual light, it necessarily acts accordingly. Therefore the way to conversion is this:

1. The soul sees the reason and foundation of spiritual carriages. Holy carriages are very reasonable, but, whatever is presented before men to persuade them, nothing will have any efficacy on them until God gives spiritual light; for they are naturally blind; they are at a loss about the reality of those things though they make a continual profession of them. But when God shines into their hearts with the light of life, they are convinced of those things that are the foundations of such carriages. They counted them as probable before, but now they are evident to them.

They see the foundations of faith in Jesus Christ. When the eyes of men are opened, they see the gracious nature of God, that He can have mercy on whom He will have mercy, that He can find in His heart to have compassion on them though they are mere creatures and incapable of being any profit to Him, though they cannot recompence Him, and though sinful creatures, whatever is the number and aggravation of their sins. They see that there is an excellency in the lovingkindness of God (Psalm 36:7).

They are convinced that none is like God in mercy, that He can abundantly pardon, that His ways are not our ways, that He is the God of all grace, that His mercy is unlimited, that His mercy passes knowledge, and so their unworthiness is no ground of discouragement. He sees also a sufficiency in Christ. Christ is precious in his eyes (1 Peter 2:7). God has made a new and living way by the blood of Christ. What tears would not do, what thousands of rams could not effect, has been done by the blood of Christ. Christ has answered all the challenges of the law and made reconciliation, bought off our punishment, and made a purchase of eternal life. He has fulfilled every jot and tittle of the law. There are unsearchable riches in Christ; there is blood enough to cleanse away all sin, a sacrifice sufficient to make atonement, price enough for our redemption, so that they may be saved without any reflection on the justice of God.

He also sees the faithfulness of God in the offers of the gospel. God invites him to come to Jesus Christ, and commands him to believe. And He has promised to accept him in a way of coming to Christ. Acts 10:43: "To Him give all the prophets witness that through His name whosoever believeth in Him shall have remission of sins." And when men see these things, they see abundant encouragements to come to Christ. These encouragements remove all difficulties; there is no one objection but is easily answered; the way is clear and plain; they see there can be no danger in relying on Christ.

They see the foundation of love. When their eyes are opened to see the gloriousness of God, they must see the reasons why they should love Him; for all the attributes of God are lovely. His grace is lovely. His mercy is very endearing in that He has a heart to pardon sin and to provide a way of salvation for sinners. His glory is renowned upon that account. Micah 7:18: "Who is a God like unto Thee, pardoning iniquity . . . ." God is mightily praised in the Church upon the account that His mercy endures forever. His justice also is a lovely, excellent property, and His name is celebrated upon that account. The Church praises Him upon that consideration. Revelation 19:2: "True and righteous are His judgments." So His holiness is lovely. The seraphim cry before Him, "Holy, holy, holy is the Lord God of Hosts." His wisdom is lovely; it is His glory that He searches the heart and tries the reins of the children of men (Jeremiah 17:10). His power is lovely. Psalm 21:13: "Be Thou exalted, Lord, by Thy own strength, so will we sing and praise Thy power."

His faithfulness is lovely. It is His commendation that His faithfulness reaches unto the clouds (Psalm 36:5). He remembers His covenant from generation to generation. He is praiseworthy because in all His attributes He therein excels all men and angels. He deserves to be loved with all the heart, with all the soul, and with all the strength. All His attributes are perfections and we have reason to delight in Him. He is so excellent on account of them that we have reason to make it the business of our lives to glorify Him. We have reason to take a complacency in Him and choose Him for our portion. When men see those attributes, they see upon what account He may justly challenge their love.

They see the foundation of humility. When this spiritual light shines into men and they see the gloriousness of God, they understand that all nations to Him are as the drop in a bucket and as dust on the scales; they are before Him as nothing, and they are less than nothing and vanity (Isaiah 49:15, 17). There is abundant reason to be thankful to Him for the least mercy, and to say, as David, that He humbled Himself to behold the things that are upon the earth (Psalm 113:6). And it becomes them to be subject to His disposals in all things, to sacrifice all their interests to His glory, and to be obedient to His voice in everything; to be abased because of their sins and lie in the dust before Him. Thus Job did in Job 42:5–6: "I have heard of Thee by the hearing of the ear, but now mine eye seeth Thee; wherefore I abhor myself and repent in dust and ashes."

When their eyes are opened to see God's glory, they see reason to lie low before Him. Psalm 8:3–4: "When I consider the heavens, the work of Thy fingers, the moon and stars that Thou hast ordained; what is man that Thou art mindful of him, and the son of man that Thou visitest him?" When men see the gloriousness of God, they see it an unreasonable thing to set up their wisdom against the wisdom of God, to set up their will against the will of God, and their interest against the glory of God. They see an infinite difference between

God and them, and that there is enough reason that
they should be humble.

2. When they see the foundation of holy carriages,
they immediately carry holily. They forthwith come to
Christ with a spirit of love and humility. When he sees
the foundation of gracious carriages, he will carry graciously. Now he acts reasonably in trusting Christ and
loving God. While he was in the dark he was unpersuadable; they might as soon prevail with a stone as
with him. But when he sees that that is a proper motive,
it will work upon his heart. When men see reason to be
afraid they will be afraid, and when they see reason to
hope they will hope. So when they see reason to believe
they will believe. Thorough conviction always prevails
on the heart. God carries on His work by light. When
suitable light is let into the heart sinners are scared,
when they see their own badness they are broken off
from their own righteousness, and when they are
turned from darkness to light they are turned from the
power of Satan to God (Acts 26:18). When God teaches
men, then they come to Christ. John 6:45: "Every man
that hath heard and learned of the Father cometh unto
Me."

*For when they see the foundation of holy carriages they are
able to carry holily.* Men cannot come to Christ unless the
Father draws them (John 6:44), but the way whereby He
draws them is by teaching them (v. 45). And when this
light is let into them they are enabled. Many sinners
are concerned to get the pardon of sin; they resolve to
come to Christ and they strive to come to Christ, but
they cannot. It seems to them a dangerous thing to venture themselves on Christ and they cannot overcome
their fears. They set many encouraging considerations

before themselves, but they cannot vanquish their fears. They dare not venture their heart upon Christ. They are as unable to come as a man who is bound with chains is to come out of prison.

It is a terror to them to continue as they are, yet they dare not cast themselves upon Christ. But when their eyes are opened to see the free grace of God and the preciousness of Christ, their fears are removed; their fetters are taken off, and now they can come, Yea, they dare not stay away from Christ; they would not for a world stay away from Christ. Satan, with all his artifices, cannot persuade them to neglect Christ. They have been in great distress, and now they see the relief that is provided for them; they are under a necessity in their own spirits to accept the call. In like manner, when they see the gloriousness of God, they are able to love Him. They were before urged in conscience to do it, and had an abundance of arguments set before them to induce them to love Him, but nothing would prevail upon them because they were strangers to the loveliness of God. But as soon as their eyes were opened to see the glorious grace of God in the gospel, they can love Him.

They made a profession before, but now they are sincere. Psalm 36:10: "Stretch forth Thy lovingkindness to them that know Thee, and Thy righteousness to the upright in heart." The heart is drawn to God; they cannot deny their love to Him. Whatever was dear to them before, now God is dearest to them. And in like manner, now they can indeed abase themselves when they see the divine excellency of God. They look on themselves as infinitely inferior to Him and lay themselves low before Him.

When they see the foundation of holy carriages, they love to carry holily. There is naturally an enmity in the heart to holy carriages. Romans 8:7: "The natural mind is enmity to God; it is not subject to the law of God, neither indeed can be." But this light makes them love holy carriages. When men see the preciousness of Christ, it mightily suits them to come to Him. They take a complacency in coming to Christ. Some men force themselves after a fashion to venture on Christ, but when they see the divine authority of the gospel they love to come to Him as the hungry man loves to eat and the thirsty to drink. Acts 16:34: "He rejoiced, believing in God." He sees that which makes it pleasant to him. He sees that God is worthy of that honor. He is a God of such grace and faithfulness that He is worthy to be trusted in, and he sees that that honor of a glorious mediator is due to Christ. He sees that it is a safe thing to come to Christ.

There is no rest anywhere else for the sole of his foot, but Christ is a sure foundation, a precious cornerstone. His heart takes contentment in relying upon Him. All the world shall not persuade him to forsake Him and make choice of any other refuge. Isaiah 45:24: "Surely one shall say, 'In the Lord have I righteousness and strength.' "

So this man loves to make the glory of God his end, and he loves to abase himself before God and look upon himself as vanity and nothing in comparison to God. The sight of the excellency of God and Christ draws his heart, and he loves these holy carriages. There was an antipathy against them in his heart before, but now God and Christ are lovely in his eyes. He now has a mind to come to Christ and to honor

God, and he will not be restrained, for such carriages are pleasant to him. The glory of God and Christ draws the heart sweetly and powerfully, and he rejoices therein.

3. This spiritual light bends the heart that way; it not only draws forth gracious actings, but leaves an impression and bias upon the heart that way. Beauty draws forth an act of love and leaves a disposition to love. This sight changes the mind and makes men judge otherwise of God and Christ than before; and it changes the heart and inclines it to carry suitably. The conviction is an abiding conviction, and so the disposition is abiding. This discovery is like a needle touching a magnet: it inclines it towards the north. When this light is let into a man he is principled to trust in Christ, to love God, and to live in a way of obedience; it prepares his heart to live in such a way. Once he is thoroughly convinced of the gloriousness of God and Christ, he is set in that way and it will abide with him as long as he lives. There is an impression left on the heart that never wears out. 2 Corinthians 3:18: "We all with open face, beholding as in a glass the glory of the Lord, are changed into the same image."

When they perform those holy carriages, they are inclined to perform them. It would be impossible to do them without an inclination to do them. If the heart were not inclined to trust in Christ, it would not trust in Him. Holy actions are never forced. Men may be under a necessity to love God and trust in Christ, but that necessity does not arise from compulsion, but from inclination. Psalm 110:3: "Thy people shall be willing in the day of Thy power."

Before, the man had an aversion to those gracious

actions; he was under the dominion of a contrary inclination. But when he does them, he is inclined to do
them; and that actual inclination leaves a habitual inclination on the heart that way. We indeed commonly
say that one act does not make a habit, but we mean
that one act does not make a more perfect habit. Habit
is distinguished from disposition, which is called *habi-
tus imperfectus*. But one act commonly leaves something
of an inclination that way. One act of love to another
person or thing disposes the heart to renew that act of
love. One act is preparation for another of the same
kind. One act of faith puts the soul into a believing
frame, and one act of humility into a humble frame. He
is more inclined to believe again than he was, and, the
clearer discovery he had of God and Christ, the more
strongly he believes, and the greater inclination remains in him to believe.

*Such men as have this spiritual discovery never utterly forget
it.* It is possible for a man to forget the first time he had
the discovery of God and Christ made to him, yet I
judge that is not ordinary. But if he forgets the time, yet
he never utterly forgets the thing. He remembers that
he has seen God and Christ to be glorious. There are
many times when he has not the actual remembrance
of it, and many times also when he has corrupt appre-
hensions concerning God and Christ and may be under the prevailings of carnal reason and unbelief; yet
he never utterly forgets what he has been convinced of,
but recovers the convictions that the gospel is true, that
Jesus Christ is an all-sufficient Savior, and so the inclination to holiness abides in his heart. 1 John 2:27: "The
anointing which ye have received of Him abideth in
you."

And though he does not have such discoveries as he has had, yet he knows he has seen it, and, accordingly, he has an inclination still to carry holily when the glory of God and Christ are out of sight. The man is sure from what he has seen that it is so, and that maintains an inclination in him to carry himself holily.

Chapter 14

There is a great difference between converting light and common illumination

Men are wont to distinguish between rational conviction and spiritual. This distinction needs to be carefully understood, for man's rational faculty is the subject both of common and spiritual conviction. We have no other faculty capable of receiving conviction but our reason. When the Spirit of God gives common conviction, he works upon reason; and when He gives spiritual conviction, He likewise works upon reason. Besides, spiritual conviction is rational conviction. Godly men act understandingly and rationally when they judge God to be worthy to be trusted, loved, and obeyed, when they judge Christ to be the eternal Son of God, an all-sufficient Savior. Yet the distinction may be allowed if it is thus explained: rational conviction is that which men by their natural reason attain, which they may gain by the force of their natural reason, improving the works and Word of God. This differs greatly from that conviction which men have by the saving work of God's Spirit.

Common illumination is of two sorts: one is from the more common improvements of natural reason, the other from more affecting discoveries wrought by a common work of the Spirit of God. There is a conviction that rises from the common improvement of natural reason. Thus men see clearly that the Protestant religion is better than the popish religion, that it must be a work of wonderful wisdom and power to make the world, that the sacrifice of the Son of God must be of great value, and that it was great love for God to give His Son to die—and hundreds of things of the like nature.

Besides these rational convictions there are affecting discoveries of divine truths by the common work of the Spirit which make, for a time, considerable impressions on the heart. Luke 14:15: "When one of them that sat at meat with Him heard these things, he said unto Him, 'Blessed is he that shall eat bread in the kingdom of God.' " Matthew 13:20: "He that received the seed into stony places, the same is he that heareth the Word and anon with joy receiveth it." 2 Peter 2:20: "For if after they have escaped the pollutions of the world through the knowledge of our Lord and Savior Jesus Christ, they are entangled therein and overcome, the latter end is worse with them than the beginning." Hebrews 6:4–6: "For it is impossible for them that were once enlightened, and have tasted of the heavenly gift, and were made partakers of the Holy Ghost, and hath tasted the good word of God and the powers of the world to come, if they fall away, to renew them again to repentance."

The two sorts of illumination are resemblances of a twofold spiritual illumination that saints have. One is by sanctified reason, whereby men are convinced of divine truths. Men understand the divine authority of the Scripture, and thereby they are assured of the truths of promises and threatenings. They are assured that God made the world, and from thence they are convinced of His eternal power and Godhead. They know that Jesus Christ is the eternal Son of God, and thereby they know the saving virtue of His blood.

The other is by special discoveries of divine truths. They are let into Christ's chambers, as the phrase is in Song of Solomon 1:4. God breaks into the heart by divine light and gives great discoveries of His faithfulness, of His holiness, His grace, the delight He takes in the sacrifice of Christ, and many other things. 2 Corinthians 4:6: "God hath shined in our hearts to give the light of the knowledge of the glory of God in the face of Jesus Christ." Both these ways seem to be intimated in Ephesians 1:17: "That God may give unto you the spirit of wisdom and revelation in the knowledge of Him."

The difference between those convictions that rise from the improvement of natural reason and those that arise from spiritual reason lies in these two things:

1. Natural reason does not reveal the certainty of divine things. Sanctified reason sees them to be sure. John 6:69: "We believe and are sure that Thou art the Christ the Son of the living God." John 17:8: "They have known that I came from Thee, and they have believed that Thou hast sent Me." Hebrews 11:1: "Faith is the evidence of things not seen." 1 Thessalonians 2:13: "They received the Word not as the word of man, but as it is indeed the Word of God." But natural reason does not reveal the certainty of divine truths. It can perceive the connection between one divine truth and another, and perceive how one thing follows certainly from another, but it does not perceive the certainty of any. Carnal men's reasoning is from supposition; they reason very rationally, but they do not see that which is the foundation of their reasoning to be certain.

Carnal men and godly men both argue from the

divine nature of Christ. Both carnal men and godly men strongly argue that if Christ is the Son of God there is a divine virtue in His sufferings, and that it is safe relying on Him. But here lies the difference: the godly man *knows* that Christ is the Son of God (Matthew 16:6), but the carnal man *supposes* that Christ is the Son of God. He says the Church believes it, the Old and New Testament give an account of it, and there are many things said that make such for the confirmation of it. He discovered the secret thoughts of men, did many miraculous works, and rose from the dead.

Upon such account he supposes Him to be the Son of God and judges it a heinous crime for any to deny it; but he does not know these things, for he is ignorant of the divine authority of the Word, and dares not venture on Christ for fear it should not be so. So it was with the Jews: they did not believe Moses (John 5:46). Thus they both argue from the types and sacraments.

The godly man argues that there were several types instituted by God to show the saving virtue of the blood of Christ, and the sacraments in the New Testament are instituted to be a memorial of Christ (1 Corinthians 11:24). The godly man argues from hence that Christ has satisfied the justice of God; that Christ was the Lamb slain from the foundation of the world (1 Corinthians 5:7). These sacrifices were only types of Christ (Colossians 2:17). And he is abundantly satisfied by these institutions that Christ is a glorious Savior.

Another man argues in like manner that God would never have appointed such signs to signify Christ if He would not have us trust in Him. He has not appointed these signs to deceive us. God would never teach His people a false way of salvation. But his wound is that he does not know certainly the divine authority of those institutions; he does not know but they were the inventions of men. So they both argue strongly from the command to believe, from the promises of salvation in a way of believing, from Christ's ascension and sitting at the right hand of God. But the carnal man is uncertain of those things that are foundations of his reasoning. He does not know but that there is some mistake. He thinks that there is a great probability of the truth of those things, but he has no assurance. His principles are grounded on an uncertain proposition, and so he knows nothing as he ought to know.

2. Carnal reason does not receive a right idea of divine things. Though godly men have the exercise of spiritual reason, they cannot find out the Almighty unto perfection. Yet they know God and Jesus Christ (John 17:3). They have a true idea of God; they know Him to be One of infinite perfection; they know Him to be a God of infinite power, grace, and faithfulness; they are convinced that He is worthy of that love, faith, and submission that He calls for. Psalm 18:3: "I will call upon God who is worthy to be praised." They know that divine honor is due to Him. Psalm 29:2: "Give unto the Lord the glory due unto His name." But carnal men do not have a right idea of God. They acknowledge that He is infinite in His perfections, and can give some description of His infinite perfections; but they do not have a right idea of His glorious nature and are not sensible what reverence and glory is due to Him. Therefore they are said to be ignorant of Him. John 4:8: "He that loveth not, knoweth not God."

The difference between those affecting illuminations that carnal men have and those discoveries that are given to godly men lies in these two particulars:

(1) The illuminations that carnal men have are affecting, but not convincing. They are many times affected with joy, so they said, "What a blessedness is it!" when Paul preached the gospel to them (Galatians 4:15). It works desires in them (Luke 14:15). And their hearts, upon that occasion, may be mightily weaned from the world and taken up about heavenly things. They may be mightily transported with zeal. The people of the Jews were so affected with Christ that they were of the mind to make Him a king.

But these illuminations do not convince them; the men remain ignorant of God, Christ, and the truth of the gospel. These flashes of light do not reveal the certainty of divine truths. The people who cry "Hosanna" today cry "Crucify Him" another time; and that is a sign they do not know Him, for had they known, they would not have crucified the Lord of glory (1 Corinthians 2:8). Many are greatly affected in the hearing of sermons who do not firmly believe what they hear. Acts 25:48: "When the Gentiles heard this, they were glad, and glorified the Word of the Lord; and as many as were ordained to eternal life believed." They were generally much affected, but it was only a select number that believed. Stony ground hearers are much affected, but not convinced.

Men are often affected with such things as they look upon as probable, but special discoveries that God makes to saints are very affecting and convincing. Godly men must be affected with those discoveries, for they are wondrous in their eyes. Psalm 119:18: "Open Thou mine eyes, that I may behold the wonderous things in Thy law." Sometimes the love of God is said to be "shed abroad in their hearts," which implies great affection (Romans 5:5).

Divine truths are of a very affecting nature. They will stir up joy, sorrow, desires, and zeal; but these discoveries do not affect them only, but also convince them. They see the glory of God. Psalm 93:2: "To see Thy power and glory, so as I have seen Thee in the sanctuary." They know the love of Christ that passes knowledge (Ephesians 3:19). When they behold the glory of God, they are convinced of the glory of God (2 Corinthians 2:18). When God shines into the hearts, He gives the light of the knowledge of the glory of God (2 Corinthians 4:6). When men see the sun, they know it is the sun; and when they see the grace and faithfulness of God, they know He is such a One. They not only see the gloriousness of mercy, holiness, and faithfulness, but that God is gracious, holy, and faithful.

(2) The illumination of carnal men does not draw forth any gracious exercises. The common discoveries that are given to carnal men have a considerable effect on them. Besides the stirring up of affections spoken of before, they have an effect upon the conversation. They many times make men to reform their lives and cast off sinful practices. 2 Peter 2:20: They "escape the pollutions of the world through the knowledge of Christ."

Sometimes they encourage men in seeking the pardon of their sins. They may have such a discovery of the happiness of heaven, of the graciousness of God, and of the mercy of God in providing a way of salvation as may greatly encourage them to continue seeking His favor. They may likewise have that effect to make men presumptuous. Men may from thence conclude their own estate to be good. They may take encouragements for assurances from the favor of God.

Men may also take occasion from them to get a false faith. If they have some discoveries of a readiness in God to pardon sinners, they may take encouragement to think that men so qualified as they, who are reformed and sorry for their sins, may be bold to venture on Christ. But those spiritual discoveries that God makes always draw forth the exercise of grace. Song of Solomon 1:4: "The king hath brought me to his chambers, we will be glad and delight in thee; the upright loveth thee." When God breaks into the heart by light, the heart is drawn forth in love, faith, and repentance. Communion is reciprocal. When God draws near to His people, it mightily stirs up a spirit of holiness. It does not only strengthen assurance, but it stirs up all grace. Job 42:5–6: "Now mine eye seeth Thee, wherefore I abhor myself, and repent in dust and ashes." Ephesians 3:19: "And to know the love of Christ that passeth knowledge; that ye might be filled with all the fulness of God." This gives great increase to grace. 2 Peter 1:2: "Grace and peace be multiplied to you through the knowledge of God and our Savior Jesus Christ."

Chapter 15

Conversion may be known

Men may have knowledge of their own conversion. The knowledge that other men have of it is uncertain, because no man can look into the heart of another and see the workings of grace there. Yet men may know that they are godly. Some ungodly think that they have grace, but that which is not cannot be known. Things that are not are called "things that do not appear" (Hebrews 11:3). That which is wanting cannot be numbered (Ecclessiastes 1:15). All converted men do not know that they are converted. Though grace is visible, yet many times it is not seen. Visible things are not alway seen—sometimes because it is night, sometimes because they are covered.

It is the calamity, and many times the iniquity, of godly men that they are ignorant of their conversion. They know that they have corruptions in them and they may know that they have grace in them. This is very evident because many godly men have known their good estate. If this knowledge had never been attained, it might more reasonably be questioned whether it was attainable. Job was abundantly satisfied. Job 10:7: "Thou knowest that I am not wicked." And he was not mistaken (Job 1:1). So David knew it in Psalm 17:15: "As for me, I shall behold His face in righteousness." So Paul says in 2 Timothy 4:7–8: "I have fought the good fight, I have finished my course, I have kept the faith. Henceforth there is laid up for me a crown of righteousness."

We do not know of one godly man in Scripture who was under darkness about his sincerity. There are some Scriptures brought to prove the contrary, especially some passages of Psalm 88, but that psalm represents to us not the particular case of Haman, but of the Church of Israel.

Further, it appears that conversion may be known because we are directed to examine ourselves in order to it. 2 Corinthians 13:5: "Examine yourselves whether you be in the faith. Prove your own selves; know you not that Jesus Christ is in you except ye be reprobates?" 2 Peter 1:10: "Give diligence to make your calling and election sure." And to what purpose should we be advised to do a thing that is not do-able? God does not advise us to impossibilities. All the commands of God are possible to be fulfilled—if not perfectly, yet they may be fulfilled. Philippians 4:13: "I can do all things though Christ, who strengtheneth me."

I shall only add the consideration that God makes many comfortable promises to those who have grace (Romans 2:7; Isaiah 3:10). But if men could not know that they have grace, that would frustrate the design of these promises; that would take away the foundation of their comfort; they would be incapable of making application of the promises to themselves. However much happiness is made over to them in those promises, yet if they could not know their own grace they must be strangers to their own happiness, and not rejoice in the good that is made over to them.

QUESTION. How may a godly man know that he has grace?

ANSWER 1. He cannot know it in a way of arguing. We come to the knowledge of many things in a way of reasoning, arguing from things known to things that are not known. Thus a man may know his justification. He may argue thus: "He who has faith in Christ is justified," or "He who has love to God is justified," or "He who loves the brethren is passed from death to life." Because there is a certain connection between these graces and a state of justification, he may argue thusly.

Thus a man may know by reasoning that he has this and that particular grace. He may argue so: "If I have the grace of faith, I have the grace of love or humility, because there is a concatenation of graces and they are inseparable one from another." But they do not know that they are gracious in this manner. The knowledge of their graces does not come in at that door.

He cannot prove it from any such acts as may proceed from other principles. A moral and religious conversation may proceed from other principles. Such a conversation is an argument to other men to be charitable, but it is no demonstration. The young man in the gospel walked exactly. Matthew 19:20: "All these things have I done from my youth." Paul was conscientious. Philippians 3:6: "Touching the righteousness that is in the law I was blameless." Such a walk may proceed from fear of hell and hope of heaven. Zeal for God does not prove it; there may be zeal where there is no love. The Jews were great enemies to Christ, yet very zealous. Romans 10:2: "I bear them record that they have a zeal for God." Paul had great zeal before he had any grace; natural conscience may produce zeal.

Great affections do not prove it. The Jews cried, "Hosanna to the Son of David!" Striving against a self-righteous spirit does not prove it. Men may strive against it, yet not mortify it. Associating with godly men does not prove it. Ahithophel was David's companion (Psalm 55:14). Sorrows for the afflictions of the Church, and desires for the conversion of souls, do not prove it. These things may be found in carnal men, and so can be no evidences of grace. Those things that are common to saints and hypocrites do not prove that a man is a saint and not a hypocrite. Men must do more than carnal men to prove that they have grace. Matthew 5:20: "Except your righteousness do exceed the righteousness of the scribes and Pharisees, you shall in no wise enter into the kingdom of heaven." That which is common to hypocrites is no sign of saintship. It is a vain thing to make that a plea which publicans may plead as well (Matthew 5:46–47). That which may rise from a corrupt principle will not prove a gracious principle; that which a beast may do will not prove something to be a man.

He cannot prove it from any such acts of providence as are common to carnal men. Some men have smiling providences and great deliverances. God is very bountiful, and many argue from thence that they are godly; but they do not argue strongly. God may smile on men here and frown on them in the day of judgment. Jude 5: "The Lord, having saved the people out of the land of Egypt, afterwards destroyed them who believed not." Prosperity is no sign of the true Church, nor of men's being members of the mystical Church.

Also, if God does the thing that men pray for, that is no argument. Many prayers are granted that are not accepted. God hears the cry of the ravens. God heard the voice of Ishmael. Sometimes God denies men's prayers because they ask amiss, but not always. Men may be instruments of a great deal of good in the church and in the commonwealth, yet be destitute of grace. Saul did a great deal of service in Israel (2 Samuel 1:24). Ministers may be instruments of the conversion of sinners and the comfort of saints, yet not be godly. There were several godly in Israel under the ministry of the scribes and Pharisees. The ravens brought meat to Elijah.

ANSWER 2. They do not know it by believing that they are godly. We know many things by faith. Hebrews 11:1: "By faith we understand that the worlds were made by the power of God. Faith is the evidence of things not seen."

Thus men know the trinity of Persons in the Godhead, that Jesus Christ is the Son of God, that he who believes in Him will have eternal life, that there is a resurrection of the dead. And if God should tell a saint that he has grace, he might know it by believing the Word of God. But it is not in this way that godly men know that they have grace. It is not revealed in the Word, and the Spirit of God does not testify it to particular persons.

Some think the Spirit does testify it to some, and they ground it on Romans 8:16: "The Spirit Himself beareth witness with our spirit that we are the children of God." They think the Spirit reveals it by giving an inward testimony to them. And some godly men think they have had experience of it, but they may easily mistake. When the Spirit of God eminently stirs up a spirit of faith and sheds abroad the love of God in the heart, it is easy to mistake it for a testimony. And that is not the meaning of Paul's words. The Spirit reveals things to us by opening our eyes to see what is revealed in the Word. But the Spirit does not reveal new truths not revealed in the Word. The Spirit reveals the grace of God in Christ, and thereby draws forth special actings of faith and love which are evidential; but it does not work in way of testimony. If God does but help us to receive the revelations in the Word, we shall have comfort enough without new revelation.

Paul's meaning is that the miraculous works of the Spirit are a witness to the Christian religion. The thing that is witnessed is that sincere Christians are the children of God, that the Christian religion is the true religion, and that all who embrace it are indeed the heirs of eternal life. And the person who witnesses is the Holy Ghost. He testifies to it by miracles and extraordinary gifts. The mighty works of the Spirit of God in the primitive times were evidences of the truth of the Christian religion; they were wrought for that very end. Hebrews 2:4: "God also bearing them witness with signs and wonders and divers miracles and gifts of the Holy Ghost." 1 Thessalonians 1:5: "Our gospel came unto you not in word only, but also in power, and in much assurance, and in the Holy Ghost."

ANSWER 3. It is by intuition or seeing grace in their own hearts. It is by consciousness, as Peter knew his love to Christ when he said, "Lord, Thou knowest all things, Thou knowest that I love Thee" (John 11:17). David knew his love to God in Psalm 116:1: "I love the Lord." Job knew his repentance in Job 42:6: "I abhor myself in dust and ashes." Paul knew that he knew Christ in 1 Timothy 1:12: "I know whom I have believed."

There is a reflecting power in man. As he can look out and see external objects, so he can look in and see his own actions. In this manner saints know the corrupt workings of their own hearts. They know their pride, worldliness, frowardness, and unbelief; and so they know their grace. In this manner they know their natural actions; they know what they think and what they think about; they know the acts of their wills, what they choose and what they refuse. They know their acts of affection: they know that they love their children, that they desire meat and drink, that they are afraid of pain and death, that they rejoice in their good things. So they may have the knowledge by intuition that they know God and Christ, that they receive the gospel, that they love God and the saints, and that they are sorry for their sins.

A godly man, understanding what it is to love God and to repent, though he cannot give an exact definition of them yet may be able by his observation to know that he does so, and may be as able to say that he loves God and believes in Christ as to say he has pride and worldliness in his own heart. There may indeed be something of more difficulty in it because many actings of grace are low and weak; on that account it may be hard to see it, just as it is hard to see the motion of water in a river when it moves very slowly. Grace is much counterfeited, and there are many actings that look like the actings of grace that are not. But sometimes grace works so powerfully that it is very visible, and men are able to distinguish between grace and the resemblance of it and be satisfied understandingly. 1 Chronicles 29:17: "As for me, in the uprightness of my heart, I willingly offered all these things."

Notwithstanding this, it may be of great use for ministers frequently to be giving signs of grace. These signs are of great use for the discovery of hypocrisy. The want of particular graces is a means to discover some.

Some may be undeceived by considering that they have not had an antecedent work of humiliation. The account of the way wherein God works grace, by the discoveries of gospel grace, may convince others. So may the allowing of pride or worldliness, and the want of doing duties out of regard for God's glory.

But signs also are of great use for the enouragement and strengthening of the saints. Sometimes the discoursing of such things draws forth the exercise of grace, and men find in themselves that which they are hearing of. So it was with Peter. The very question whether he loved Christ or not kindled a spirit of love in him that assured him he loved Christ (John 21:17). Sometimes the explication of the sign helps men to see it more clearly. They were at a loss, but when it is clearly laid open it helps them to see it. Besides, it brings to remembrance what they formerly felt; and so it brings joy and renews their comfort. Moreover it helps them against many temptations. They are under fears because of the providence of God and because of corrupt workings of heart; but when they hear that complacency of God and the sight of the glory of Christ are signs of a good estate, that satisfies them, and it is a relief to them under their temptations.

Chapter 16

The grace given in conversion is imperfect

The grace given in conversion, like other qualities, admits of innumerable degrees, and is very imperfect in the best of the people of God. Godly men are far from pretending to perfection. Job 9:20: "If I say I am perfect, it shall also prove me perverse." Hence we find lamentations of some of the choicest men who have been in the world. Proverbs 30:2: "Surely I am more brutish than any man, and have not the understanding of a man." Romans 7:23–24: "I see another law in my members, bringing me into captivity. O wretched man that I am, who shall deliver me from the body of this death?" The sorrowful falls of David, Solomon, Hezekiah, Jonah, and Peter are sufficient demonstrations of this, and the warfare that every godly man experiences. Galatians 5:17: "The flesh lusteth against the spirit, and the spirit against the flesh, and these are contrary the one to the other, so that ye cannot do the things that ye would." Especially, grace at conversion is very small. If after twenty or thirty years of growth it is very defective, it must be very small at first.

There are many reasons why God suffers much sin to remain in His people while they remain in this world.

1. That the work of sanctification may be so carried on that they may be in continual need of justification and pardon. The pardoning of the very sins that men committed in their unconverted state is a great mani-

77

festation of the riches of His grace and the virtue of the
blood of Jesus Christ. But God day by day pardons the
repeated iniquities of His people. He forgives men
thousands of times, though they have abused mercy,
broken vows, and fallen from resolutions. This wonderfully commends the grace of God and the sacrifice of
Jesus Christ. If there were not experiences of it, it would
be difficult to conceive that God would be willing to do
so. These are mighty instances of the unsearchable
depth of mercy that is in the heart of God, and they
lead me to say, with Micah 7:18, "Who is a God like unto
Thee, that pardoneth iniquity, and passeth by the transgression of the remnant of His heritage, and retaineth
not His anger forever, because He delighteth in
mercy?"

2. Because they live among carnal men, scattered up
and down among unconverted men. If their grace was
perfect, they would not be fit to live together. It would
be known who was godly and who was ungodly, which
would fill families, towns, and countries with temptation. Godly men would be put to it to bear the carriages
of the ungodly, and ungodly men would not know how
to bear the carriages of the godly. It would fill all soci-
eties with disquietment and trouble.

3. Because this is suitable to those administrations
that God has appointed in His house. And the worship
that God has appointed is suited both for the conversion of sinners and the building up of saints, to promote their humiliation and recovery from backslidings
and relief under temptations. If godly men were perfect,
they and ungodly men would not be fit to join together
in confession or petition. The ordinances that God has
appointed are not fit to be attended by men who have

attained to a perfection in grace.

Some saints attain to greater perfection in grace than others. This is not always in proportion to the time since their conversion, but according to the improvement of their time. It is said of the Thessalonians that their faith grew exceedingly and their charity abounded (2 Thessalonians 1:3). Some have more grace at first conversion than others, and some may grow more in a year than others in seven. And though it would be a presumptuous thing to determine the degree of grace any have attained to in this life, yet it seems probable that saints do not ordinarily, if ever, attain to such measures of grace but that they have more corruption than grace.

It seems to be but a little grace compared with corruption that God's choice servants attain unto. It is said of the angel of Philadelphia, "Thou hast a little strength, and hast kept My word and hast not denied My name" (Revelation 3:8). And the experience of the people of God seems to confirm this. Sin easily besets them (Hebrews 12:1). Corruption is like a fountain that is continually sending forth its waters. Temptations quickly infest. Pride and worldliness, discontent and unbelief, are very ready to work; and there is a great backwardness to spiritual duties, to faith and love, and to submit to the sovereignty of God. Men's enjoyments are so dear to them that they have great difficulty resigning them up to the pleasure of God. There is much formality that attends duties of religion, and there is much spiritual blindness, igorance of God and Jesus Christ.

Neither does it make against this assertion that some of the people of God have a very exemplary conversation; for there are many other principles that join in with grace to effect this: natural conscience, a regard for one's reputation, a good temper, principles of morality, hope of reward and fear of punishment. If an exemplary conversation were an argument that men had more grace than corruption, how does it come about that some men have not one spark of grace to carry exemplarily? A good conversation is sometimes only the effect of nature improved.

USE. The use of this discourse is of exhortation to labor to be converted. Conversion is a glorious change and will issue in eternal glory. You may observe many men striving with all their might to add to their worldly comforts; they spare no pains, but are laying out themselves indefatigably to mend their accomodations and increase their enjoyments here. But it will turn to better account for you to labor after a work of regeneration. I do not advise you to effect it, for it is beyond your power. When the prophet said, "Make ye a new heart and a new spirit, for why will ye die, O house of Israel," he intended that the nation should get a disposition to reform. But though you cannot effect this yourselves, yet you can labor in it.

You may not indulge yourselves in negligence, excusing yourselves for your impotence. God expects that you should strive to enter in at the strait gate (Luke 13:24), that you press into the kingdom of God, and be violent that you may obtain it. It is well worth your while to be engaged in this matter, and to give yourselves no rest until you are converted. If God gives you many outward comforts, let them not satisfy you. Cry out that one thing is lacking. "What will it profit a man if he should gain the whole world and lose his own soul?" (Matthew 16:26).

Some content themselves with the reputation of being converted, but it is not the *name*, but the *thing* that you must crave. Some things are to be sought with a great deal of indifference; this must be bought with agony of spirit. You must cry for wisdom, and lift up your voice for understanding; you must seek it as silver and search for it as for hidden treasures (Proverbs 2: 3–4).

This is a thing of such necessity that you may not delay striving after it, and whatever occasions you have you must allow no excuses. Whatever difficulties you meet with you must never be discouraged. If others should faint, you must hold out. Avoid everything that has a tendency to hinder success. Shun all things that will stupify or divert or discourage; practice everything that is proper and serviceable to your conversion. Do not think it much to deny your pleasures, to forego lawful liberties, to let slip worldly opportunities, to endure hardship, to endure terrors. Spare no cost, no pains, so you may be converted.

Motives

1. A natural condition is a very sinful condition. Unconverted men are ungodly men. There are but two sorts of men in the world: godly and ungodly. All ungodly men are utterly destitute of holiness; their natures are corrupted; they are servants of Satan and live in a way of rebellion against God. In this respect they are worse than the beasts of the earth: their natures are superior, but they are more corrupt than brute crea-

tures. Upon this account they are vile in the eyes of
God. If any of them are in an honorable station outwardly, yet they are abominable to God. Some think
that God takes delight in them because of His bounty
to them, but they are mistaken. God looks on them as
filthy and abominable. They are a continual provocation to God. Psalm 7:11: "God is angry with the wicked
every day."

(1) Your hearts are full of sin. Some men carry
themselves more orderly and religiously than others,
but their hearts are desperately wicked (Ecclessiastes
9:3). The hearts of the sons of men are full of evil. Some
are under greater divine restraints than others, but the
same abominations that break out in other men are in
them. They have the seeds of all wickedness in them.
Romans 8:7: "The natural mind is enmity against God."
They are enemies to the authority of God, the wisdom
of God, the power of God, and the justice of God—yea,
to the very being of God. They have a preparedness to
all the wickedness that is perpetrated in the world if
God did not restrain them. As face reflects face in the
water, so does the heart of man reflect a man.

Many times, if they behold beforehand what workings of heart they should have, they would say as
Hazael, "Is thy servant a dog that he should do this
thing?" (2 Kings 8:13). If they were in Cain's circumstances, and God would suffer them, they would do as
badly as he did. If they were in Pharaoh's circumstances
and left of God, they would be as cruel, false, and hard-
hearted as he was. If they were in the like circumstances
with Doeg, though they condemn him for his
hypocrisy, flattery, and cruelty, they would do every whit
as bad as he. If they were in the like circumstances as

Judas was, whatever indignation they have against him, they would be as false and impudent and as traitorous as he. Yea, if they were under the circumstances that the fallen angels were, they would be as very devilish as they.

A serpent, when numbed with cold, is a serpent still. A lion in a grate is the same fierce creature that he was before. A swine that is washed is a swine still. Some of them have a regular conversation, but a spirit of uncleanness, intemperance, profaneness, atheism, and blasphemy is not mortified. That original sin which reigns in every natural man is the fountain of every abomination. Every natural man is overrun with the leprosy of sin from head to foot. He has not one spark of goodness in him; all his faculties are corrupted utterly; his understanding is blind. He talks of God, but is quite a stranger to Him. His will is miserably corrupted. He prefers vain and base things before God. All his affections are quite out of order. His whole soul is like a dead carcass, like a heap of carrion, loathsome and noisesome, and God may justly abhor him, which evidently shows a great necessity of his conversion.

(2) Your lives are full of sin. Men, in their natural condition, are guilty of a world of sin. Some of them live in a way of profaneness. They set their mouth against the heavens (Psalm 73:9). Some live in the ways of sensuality and wallow like swine in the mire. Some live in ways of injustice; they are beasts of prey. Some are mere earthworms, seeking a heaven upon the earth. They are under the curse of the serpent: Death shall be the serpent's meal. And such of them as are addicted to morality and religion are serving their lusts therein.

The most orderly natural men live an ungodly life.

In all the works of their calling they carry themselves sinfully. Proverbs 21:4: "The plowing of the wicked is sin." In all their relations they carry themselves sinfully. Under all providences they live ungodly. When they eat and drink, they do it not as they should, for God's glory, but are eating and drinking damnation to themselves. Yea, their very religion is iniquity (Isaiah 1:15). Their hearts are set upon carnal things. Romans 8:5: "They that are after the flesh do mind the things of the flesh." Though some of them whose consciences are enlightened are reforming their lives and crying to God for the pardon of sin, yet they are minding carnal things as well as others; they are setting up their own righteousness and nourishing the pride of their spirits (Revelation 3:17). They do not mind the spiritual enjoyments of heaven, but the bodily enjoyments. They pray for holiness, but oppose it. John 5:42: "They have not the love of God in them." They praise God because of His excellency, but they do not believe Him to be such a one; it is a burden to them that they suspect it, and they wish He were not such a one. They wish God did not see their hearts and had no power to avenge Himself.

There is nothing but hypocrisy in all they do. They confess their sins and bewail their iniquities, but they have no godly sorrow. They put up earnest requests for holiness, but do not sincerely desire it. They strive against sin and all the while cherish it. They have pangs of affection, but no love. They have some affection to saints, but hate real holiness. They are zealous against some sins, but hate none. They are striving for salvation, but refuse the offers of it.

Sometimes God tries them by convincing them of

the great danger of their damnation, and they show a dreadful, wicked, and rebellious spirit that they are scared to see themselves. There is a great deal of the spirit of the devil in them. Upon this account, there is great need of their conversion.

2. If you are not converted, you will perish forever. It may be that God will bring great calamity on you in this world on that account. He may curse you in your estate, in your body, or in your relations. It may be He may shorten your days. But however that may be, you *will* be damned. If you live here among many who go to heaven, yet you will go to hell. You may possibly enjoy many good things here from the bounty of God, but you will not find mercy from the Lord in that day. You may flatter yourselves with the hopes of heaven, but when your case comes to be determined you will be sent to hell. John 3:3: "Except a man be born again, he cannot see the kingdom of God." If you have other qualifications that are commendable and honorable, yet you will be rejected. Moral qualifications which heathens may attain to will not prepare you for heaven. If you pity the poor, God will not pity you. If you shed many tears, they will not quench the fires of God's wrath. You were born children of wrath, and if you continue in your natural condition you will remain under the wrath of God.

God will not take men to heaven who continue in a state of enmity to Him. If the choicest men on earth pray for your salvation, God will not hear them. All unconverted men are ungodly men. If they are honest men, if they are sober men, if they are religious men, if they are zealous men, yet they are ungodly men; and they shall be driven from light to darkness and chased

out of the world. If they are not converted they are not
pardoned, and there will be no place for them in
heaven. Matthew 18:3: "Except ye be converted, and become as little children, ye shall not enter into the
kingdom of heaven."

And can you content yourselves to be in a perishing
condition? Can you stand still till the wrath of God
overtakes you? What will it signify for you to eat and
drink and get land and cattle, and spend away a few
years after some troublesome manner, and then sink
down into the bottomless pit? A dying time will come;
can you think of it without horror? Will it not be a burden too heavy for you? It is an awful thing to chink of
the damnation of neighbors; and can you bear the
thoughts of your own damnatio⁻.? One would think you
should not be able to take any comfort in your choicest
enjoyments because it is likely to be your portion at last
to lie down in sorrow.

Do you not think that Cain, Saul, and Judas, and the
sinners in the old world were in a doleful estate; and
are you willing to be among the rest? Can you bear to
hear that sentence from Matthew 25:41: "Depart ye
cursed?" Is not the wrath of God too heavy for you? Is
not hellfire too hot for you? You shun reproach, you
avoid pain, you hate poverty, and are you able to bear
hell? When you come to lie in torment, can you satisfy
yourself that you have had your good things? Will you
be able to applaud yourself as having acted the part of a
wise man? Will you glory in your wisdom, and bless
yourself for loitering away your time? One hour's experience of the pains of hell will effectually teach you that
peace with God is worth your care and labor, and that
working out your salvation is no intolerable burden.

If the doctrine of hell were a dream, if when you died your soul would be resolved into its first principles, if there were no hell but in the imaginations of doting men, you might bless yourself in that way. But if there is a God in heaven who will execute vengeance upon ungodly men, your neglecting to get into a converted condition is the highest madness and folly. You act like the man possessed with the devil who cast himself sometimes into the fire and sometimes into the water. One would think that you should be saying to yourself as did they in Isaiah 33:14: "Who among us can dwell with the devouring fire?"

Are you patient enough, are you strong enough, are you stout enough to bear everlasting burnings? Are you more hardy than the devils, who believe and tremble? When men are in great pains, they hope that they will abate after awhile. When they have sorrows, they hope for a change afterwards. But what will you have to comfort you when your miseries are everlasting? When death shall come upon you, can you bid it welcome? You would rather be turned into nothing than be turned into hell. Is it not better to take pains that you may escape than loiter away your time until destruction comes upon you like an armed man?

3. If you are converted, God will bestow eternal life upon you. If a man is indeed converted, yet he may have great afflictions in this world. Though God many times rewards men with outward blessings, yet that is a more arbitrary way; and He mixes many afflictions with them. So it was with Jacob, Job, and David; but converted men shall have eternal life. He will bestow some other things of great consequence upon them. He will hear their prayers, accept their services, and have commu-

nion with them. And at last He will bestow eternal life upon them. James 5:20: "He that converteth a sinner from the error of his way shall save a soul from death." Acts 3:19: "Repent and be converted that your sins may be blotted out, when the time of refreshing shall come from the presence of the Lord." Acts 26:18: "To turn them from darkness to light, and from the power of Satan unto God, that they may receive the forgiveness of sins, and an inheritance among them that are converted."

After they are converted, they may do that which is very provoking to God, and God may execute fatherly anger upon them. But they shall not miss eternal life thereby; there is no falling from a state of adoption or justification. Conversion will issue in glorification. John 4:14: "The water that I shall give him shall be in him a well of water, springing up into eternal life." It is a great thing to go to heaven, but this shall be the portion of all who are converted. The generality of men will fall short of heaven, but no converted man will. Wealthy man, gifted men, honorable men, and religious men may, but converted men shall not. Romans 8:30: "Whom He called, them He also justified, and whom He justified, them He also glorified."

And can you content yourselves to lose such a benefit? If your salvation is secured, then you may bless yourself; you may rejoice in hope of the glory of God. If you are under affliction, if you hear of wars and troubles, you may say with David in Psalm 46:1–2: "The Lord is my strength and refuge, a very present help in time of trouble; therefore will I not fear, though the earth be removed."

When you look into the Bible, there you may read

your title. When you hear the Word, you will hear abundant matter of consolation. When you are exercised with your corruptions, you may comfort yourselves with the fact that after awhile Christ will present you without spot or blemish. When Satan is tempting, you may rejoice that God will tread Satan under your feet shortly. When you mourn under the withdrawings of God, you may be refreshed with the consideration that ere long you shall behold His face in righteousness. When you are afflicted with your ignorance, you may rejoice in the knowledge that you shall be wise like the angels of God. When you are afflicted with a dull, crazy, distempered body, you may remember to your comfort that Christ will change your vile body and make it like His own most glorious body.

You desire such and such earthly comforts, but you have reason to be more indifferent about those; they will not make you happy if you have them, and the lack of them will not make you miserable. Can you be content to have your portion in this life while others have heaven and eternal glory?

Christ has died for the salvation of sinners. God has appointed ordinances to persuade men to be saved. And is it not worth your while to labor in it? If you get into a state of salvation, you shall not need be afraid of death; death, that is a terror to the princes of this world, need be no terror to you. You may look upon it as a conquered enemy. You may say, "O death, where is thy sting? O grave, where is thy victory?" Does it not make too much of your pains and trouble in striving for conversion? Heaven will make amends for all. Men who are rejoicing in worldly things walk in a vain show; but heaven is not a little thing. It is a wonder that God does not say, "It is too much to give heaven to such as you." We should be far from saying it is too little for us. It becomes you to say, "Let who will take the world, so long as I may obtain heaven."

There may be some joy in earthly things, but in God's presence is fullness of joy. They who enter into heaven enter into the joy of their Lord. They are blessed to whom it shall be said, "Inherit the kingdom prepared for you." If it is good to have meat, drink, and clothing, to be with Christ is far better.

4. There is much difficulty in the way of conversion. Thus we are taught by Christ in Matthew 7:14: "Strait is the gate and narrow is the way that leadeth unto life, and few there be that find it." Indeed, we read of some who have been converted all of a sudden, who took no great pains to be converted (the jailer in Acts 16, the woman of Samaria in John 4, and many of the Gentiles in Acts 13). It may possibly be so now with some on their sickbeds; and therefore there is sufficient encouragement for ministers to advise them and pray for them. God can suddenly let in so much light as is sufficient for their conversion. But if God does not wonderfully prevent it, ordinarily there is much difficulty in the way. Christ Jesus makes that argument for men to labor after it in Luke 13:24: "Strive to enter in at the strait gate." There are abundant difficulties in the way, so that unless persons labor in it they are never likely to be converted. Many seek and are not able to enter. Their ignorance makes the work difficult; they are in great danger of taking wrong paths; their reason misleads them; they get out of the right way, and so make a great deal of work for themselves.

Their love to carnal things makes the work difficult;

there is much opposition from a worldly spirit that makes them dull and sluggish, that swallows up a great deal of time, that fills them full of care.

Their pride is a great hindrance; it fills with conceits of their own sufficiency. Their fearfulness creates a great deal of difficulty and they are ready to be discouraged. They have a great deal of frowardness, and they are ready to be disgusted and prejudiced. The blindness of their minds hinders them from seeing their way. A spirit of self-love leads them in wrong paths. And Satan is laying many snares for them. He works on their corruptions and takes all occasions to strengthen their lusts.

There is a great deal of difficulty in the way of reformation. It is a great while, sometimes, before they will forsake their evil ways. If they do many things, like Herod they will stick at some particulars; they will bear many a gird of conscience before they will reform some things; they have their excuses and evasions. If they thoroughly reform and do duties of self-denial, it is not brought about without a great deal of terror. His mother's curse made Micah to reform His injustice (Judges 17). They will not cast away their idols of gold without a great deal of terror (Isaiah 2:20–21). Many persons deal very deceitfully a great while about the work of reformation. They pretend to reformation when they are not thoroughly reformed; their moisture is turned into the drought of summer before they will comply.

And there is a great deal of difficulty in the work of humiliation. They are called to come to Jesus Christ, but they will try other methods first, and go about to establish their own righteousness (Romans 10:3). They dare not venture upon Christ till they have made their hearts better. They say they are not papists, yet they have great dependence upon their works. Sometimes they fancy they are converted, and please themselves that God is bound in faithfulness to pardon them upon Christ's account. Proverbs 30:12: "There is a generation that are pure in their own eyes, yet are not cleansed from their filthiness." Sometimes they think they have taken a great deal of pains and have done a great deal of service, and they can't conceive that it would be a fair thing for God to cast them off. It looks very hard for God to despise all they have done and reject them. Isaiah 58:3: "Wherefore have we fasted, and Thou seest us not? Wherefore have we afflicted our souls, and Thou takest no knowledge?"

Sometimes they take notice of the meltings of their hearts, their desires for holiness, their delights in Sabbaths. And it seems to them as if God could not be very angry, as if they had melted the heart of God into compassions, and made Him more easy and willing to pardon them; as if God could not find in His heart to cast them off; as if their lamentations could force the pity of God. And when their hearts appear worse, they nourish a hope to bring them too, and take a great deal of pains to work upon such frames as may lay bonds on God to save them. They are told that it is in the pleasure of God to bestow mercy or to deny it; but they dread the thought of that and try twenty conclusions before they will submit to God.

They strive greatly to bring God under a necessity to save them. They make objections against God's prerogative. They strive to bring their hearts into a kind of submission, making a righteousness of it, and would submit to prevent submission. There are so many diffi-

culties in the way that men need to be greatly concerned, and to be working out their salvation with fear
and trembling. There is so much difficulty that many
times it is long, and with great struggling, that they fi-
nally obtain. Some never obtain. After awhile they grow
discouraged and think it is to no purpose; they grow
cool and indifferent; they start some other design and
by degrees are entangled in the pollutions of the world
again; they become like the salt that has lost its savor.

Some persons settle at length in a way of carnal confidence, building their hopes upon the sand. There are
many pharasaical professors who glory in themselves
and speak peace to themselves when there is no peace.
They are deceived with false appearances of love and
faith, and think themselves something when they are
nothing. Some others spend their days like Israel in the
wilderness: they wander about from mountain to hill,
seeking rest and finding none. They beat upon the
coast, but never enter into the harbor. They are striving, and death comes and puts an end to all their
hopes. But those who get into a converted condition
have many difficulties to grapple with before they obtain, and they are under a necessity to labor much in it.
Matthew 11:12: "The kingdom of heaven suffereth violence, and the violent take it by force."

5. It is hopeful that, if you strive, you may obtain. He
who plows, plows in hope. If there were no hope of obtaining, men would not be prevailed with to seek. Hope
made the king of Nineveh seek the favor of God (Jonah
3:9). Despair kills the heart, cramps the powers of nature, and makes men deaf to persuasions; but hope
makes men pray, strive, run ventures, and endure hardship. Hopes of a cure make the sick use medicines.

Hopes of a harvest make the husbandman to till his ground. Hopes of arriving at the port make the mariner hoist his sails. Hopes of victory make the soldier fight. And God encourages men to seek Him from the hopes of success. Isaiah 55:6: "Seek ye the Lord while He may be found; call ye upon Him while He is near." Men are wont to give way to a discouraged spirit, partly from dark appearances, partly from frowardness, and partly from slothfulness. But they do very ill, for it is hopeful that they may obtain.

(1) For God will bestow converting grace upon some. We are indeed assured that all will not obtain. We are also assured that some will obtain, for there are a number of men whose names are written in the book of life. There may be more of them in one age than in another, more of them in one professing country and town than in another; but all who are elect shall obtain (Romans 11:7). There is a number who are redeemed by Christ, for whom He designedly shed His blood. He laid down His life for His sheep (John 10:15). God would never have sent Him into the world but that designed to convert and save many sinners through Him. He has promised to Jesus Christ the salvation of many. Isaiah 49:6: "I have given Him to be a light unto the Gentiles, and salvation to the ends of the earth." Psalm 72:17: "Men shall be blessed in Him, and all nations shall call Him blessed." This is the promise spoken of in Titus 1:2: "In hope of eternal life, which God that cannot lie promised before the world began." God has made a donation of an eternal kingdom to Christ. Matthew 16:18: "The gates of hell shall not prevail against the Church."

The work of conversion shall be carried on in all

ages. Ordinances shall not be in vain. Matthew 28:19–
20: "Go, teach all nations, baptizing them; and lo I am
with you even to the end of the world." When God
sends sowers to sow, some seed shall fall on good
ground. The gospel is as a net that gathers some good
fish and some bad. As other great works of God are
continued, so this work of conversion shall continue in
all ages. Though Satan has a kingdom in the world, yet
Christ will always have a kingdom here as well as he.

(2) There is ground to hope that He will bestow
saving grace on you. You are under the means of grace;
accordingly the ministers of the gospel should hope
for you and, accordingly, take pains with you. It would
be a very sinful thing if they should be discouraged
about you and neglect to teach, warn, and direct you.
Paul tells us that he warned all his hearers (Acts 20:31).
And as there is ground for the minister to take encouragement to endeavor your conversion, so there is
ground for you to be encouraged to strive for your own
conversion.

If it were beyond the power of God to convert, or beyond the grace of God to pardon you, then you would
have reason to be discouraged. Men may not expect
impossibilities, but God can renew His image within
you. The soul of a man is a suitable subject for grace;
and as long as the faculties of the soul remain a capacity to be gracious remains. Your corruptions are acci-
dental, and so may be mortified. Your mind cannot be
so blind as to be incapable of light. Your heart cannot
be so hard as to be incapable of being made soft. If your
corruptions are very strong, omnipotence can overcome them. Matthew 19:26: "With God all things are
possible."

Neither is it beyond the grace of God to pardon you. It is great folly to set limits to that which is infinite. God's grace exceeds man's sinfulness. His thoughts are not as our thoughts, nor His ways as our ways, but are high above them as the heavens are above the earth. Indeed, if God had revealed that He would not pardon you, that would cut off all hope; but there is no such thing in the Word. God says in His Word that His Spirit would not always strive with flesh (Genesis 16:3), but that signifies that He would wait only a hundred and twenty years and then bring the flood. He says that the heart of the people shall be made fat (Isaiah 6:10), but that was a national judgment; particular persons might be converted for all that. Sometimes God swore concerning Israel that they should not enter into His rest (Psalm 95:11), but there is no such thing said concerning you. God sometimes pronounces that curse, "Let him that is unjust be unjust still, and him that is filthy be filthy still" (Revelation 22:11), but He is using means with you still.

You may take notice of some dark appearances in providence: that you are of such an age, that God has refused hitherto to hear your prayers, that in the days when many have heard the voice of the Son of God you have been left. But it is unwarranted and presumptuous without Scripture or reason to draw any dark conclusions from thence.

(3) If you are striving there is a great deal of hope that you will obtain. If men are striving and will not be discouraged, it is very hopeful that they will in time be converted—especially if they are directed aright and not flattered, for diligent seeking is God's way. God's voice unto men is, "Seek ye My face" (Psalm 27:8). So

"seek the Lord and His face, seek His strength ever-more" (Psalm 105:4). There is hope that God will own men when they take the directions of His Word. Though natural men, when they seek conversion, al-ways do it with a selfish and hypocritical spirit, and God does not accept it as service to Himself, yet it is not strange that He should bless His own appointments. Indeed, seeking God diligently, reforming men's lives, searching into the way of salvation, has a great ten-dency to promote salvation; for it takes men off of their sinful practices and worldly designs that hindered them from getting into the way of life. They are search-ing into those things that will conduce to their conver-sion.

Besides, when men are earnestly seeking after that, it is a sign that the Spirit of God is at work with them. And the Spirit has promised to make the means of grace effectual. John 16:7–8: "If I depart, I will send the Comforter to you; and when He is come He will reprove the world of sin, of righteousness, and of judgment." And when He intends to convert, His way is, first, to convince of sin; and when He convinces of sin, many times it is in order to conversion. And indeed many persons have had experience that in a way of laboring after conversion God has shown mercy to them, while others who have been careless and slight have contin-ued in an unconverted condition. Many who have been striving to enter in at the strait gate have obtained; and it is always so that where there is in any place an earnest desire to be seeking peace with God many ob-tain mercy. And if that spirit should continue longer, many more might obtain, according to Matthew 11:12, "The kingdom of heaven suffereth violence, and the violent take it by force."

6. If you should obtain conversion, you would not be in an unconverted state again for all the world. A man who has a fair estate may be very willing to exchange for another; but if you were converted you would despise lordships and principalities in comparison thereof. The glory of the world might possibly be a temptation, but you would never be willing to change a converted estate for all the glory of the world. When you are called to mind the doleful condition of such men, you would look upon them as objects of commiseration. Their jollity, wealth, and grandeur would not reconcile you to their condition. You would remember the wormwood and the gall. You would think of the vanity of their hopes, the dolefulness of their death, and their eternal confusion; and their estate would be a matter of horror to you. Jeremiah dreaded to return to the house of Jonathan.

Whatever enjoyments you had—pedigree, estate, honorable offices—upon this account you would call yourself happy: that you were converted. When you considered what it delivered you from and what it entitled you to, you would say, as as the apostle did of peace with God, that it passes all understanding. Conversion opens a door to the richest treasures. He thinks with himself, "What a comfort it is to have peace with God, to be delivered from the fear of death, to be delivered for eternity."

God is his, Christ is his, and heaven is his. He wishes it were so with others. Acts 26:29: "I wish that others were such as I am, except these bonds." Men who obtain great things in the world are never content, but when they are converted they say, "It is enough." You would say, "Others eat the fat and drink the sweet. Some have great incomes, some have honorable offices, some have glittering attire. But, as David says in Psalm 17:15, 'As for me, I shall behold Thy face in righteousness. I shall be satisfied when I awake with Thy likeness.' "

The Way to Know Sincerity and Hypocrisy Cleared Up

"Every one that loveth is born of God and knoweth God. He that loveth not, knoweth not God."
1 John 4:7–8

Godliness is a thing of great concern. The acceptance of services, the hearing of prayers, and the salvation of the soul depends upon it. And because it is of such moment, the comfort of men much depends upon the knowledge of it. But there is a great deal of darkness in the minds of men about it. Many times godly men have scruples, and sometimes great fears, that they are not godly. They often sit in judgment on themselves and are at a loss what sentence to pronounce. And some ungodly men have great hopes that they are in a good estate and steal comforts that do not belong to them. Some cannot see their way to condemn themselves, and some give judgment for themselves. But the apostle here directs the one sort and the other in the determination of their condition.

First, he tells us how a godly man may know his godliness. He who sees the workings of the grace of love in himself, he who sees more or fewer actings of that grace, may conclude for himself that he is born of God, has had a work of regeneration, that the gospel has had a saving efficacy on his heart, that he has the spiritual knowledge of God, and that his eyes have been opened to see the glory of God.

Second, he tells us how hypocrites may know their hypocrisy. He who does not love, who lives in the omission of love, who has nothing of the working of that spirit, who lives in the neglect of it, has not the spiritual knowledge of God, whatever pretences he makes, this casts the case against him. The like we may say with respect to every other grace: He who believes on Jesus Christ, who loves God, who has godly sorrow, is born of God. But he who does not believe in Christ, who loves not God, who has not godly sorrow, knows not God, whatever professions he makes.

Men may know their hypocrisy only by their course of life; but their sincerity only by particular acts.

There are two sorts of professors, saints and hypocrites. Some are compared to wheat and some to chaff. Matthew 3:12: "He will gather the wheat into His garner; but He will burn up chaff with unquenchable fire." Some are compared to stony and thorny ground, some to good ground (Matthew 13:20). Some have a wedding garment, some have not (Matthew 22:11). Some are compared to wise, some to foolish virgins (Matthew 25:1–2). Some are compared to men who build upon a rock, others to men who build upon the sand (Matthew 7:24ff). And many persons are studying this question, of what sort they are. This doctrine resolves it.

PROPOSITION 1: Hypocrisy is to be known only by their course of life. Men know it only by their walk.

For the clearing of this, consider:

I. Particular acts of sin are no evidence of hypocrisy.

1. Many internal acts of sin are no evidence of hypocrisy. Every godly man has a corrupt principle re-

maining in him, and that principle does not lie still; but is busy and active. Though it is mortified, yet it is full of life. Hebrews 12:1: "Lay aside every weight, and the sin that doth so easily beset us." It is like a fountain, always springing up. Galatians 5:17: "The flesh lusts against the spirit." Romans 7:21: "I find a law, that when I would do good, evil is present with me." The choicest saints every day find the stirrings of corruption. If they are alone, if they are in company, if they are in the works of their calling, if they are exercising themselves in the duties of religion, they are always haunted with a corrupt heart. They have a multitude of evil thoughts, desires, delights, fears, sorrows. Unbelief is often stirring; so pride and worldliness, frowardness and envy. There are many stirrings of sin that they do not perceive; but an abundance falls under their observation. A corrupt principle will stir upon all occasions; every thing that occurs will awaken it. Therefore saints are warned to keep their hearts with all diligence (Proverbs 4:23). And godly men have great occasion every day to repent, and to say as Paul in Romans 7:24: "O wretched man that I am, who shall deliver me from the body of this death!"

2. Many external acts of sin are no evidence of hypocrisy. Men have much more command of their words and outward actions than of their thoughts and the inward workings of their hearts. Yet godly men are often guilty of external sins. They commit many sins in words. James 3:8: "The tongue is an unruly evil." Many times their words savor of vanity, pride, unbelief, and uncontentedness. And they are often guilty of other external sins. Psalm 19:12: "Who can understand his errors?" Every corruption is running them into trans-

gression, sometimes omitting duty, sometimes committing sin. They are guilty of many sins of ignorance. Men who understand general rules often fail in applying them to particular cases. There are many proud, worldly, froward carriages that they are not aware of, and are ready to justify. And many sins are committed through inadvertency; they are hurried through fear or passion or pride, and consider not at the time, but presently after they see it and are sorry for it.

3. An act of gross transgression is no evidence. Gross transgressions are not the ordinary spots of God's children, but grace is no certain preservation from them. Mortified corruption may run a man into such transgression as many natural men were never guilty of. Gross transgressions are of such a nature that they seem to be inconsistent with grace. But as a man who has corruption in him may do choice acts of holiness, so a man who has grace in him may commit gross acts of sin. If a man's nature is much weakened, yet in a fit he may act very strongly. So if men's corruptions are much weakened, yet they may have fits wherein they may act very powerfully. It is an idle thing to think that such things are impossible as several times have come to pass. Noah's intemperance, Lot's incest, David's adultery, and Peter's denying of Christ are unanswerable arguments that gross transgression is no evidence of a hypocrite. It is no wonder if a gross transgression should make a man suspect his godliness, but it is no evidence. If God withdraws from a godly man, his grace will not prevent gross transgression. Natural conscience often preserves men, but grace does not always preserve men from gross sin.

II. A course of sin is an evidence of hypocrisy. If a man makes a profession of religion, and lives in a way of sin against the light of his conscience, he is a hypocrite. He who makes a profession and contradicts it in his conversation is a hypocrite. Titus 1:16: "They profess that they know God, but in works they deny Him." He who pretends to godliness and turns aside to crooked ways is a hypocrite; for those who are really godly live in a way of obedience. Psalm 119:1–3: "Blessed are the undefiled in the way, that walk in the way of the Lord, they also do no iniquity." Luke 1:6: "They were both righteous before God, walking in all the commandments and ordinances of the Lord blameless."

But such as live in ways of sin are dissemblers, for all such will be rejected in the day of judgment. Matthew 7:23: "Depart from Me, ye that work iniquity." The like we have in Luke 13:27. If men *live* in a way of disobedience, they do not *love* God; for love will make men keep God's commands. 1 John 5:3: "Herein is love, that we keep His commands, and His commands are not grievous." If men live in a way of disobedience they have not a spirit of faith, for faith sanctifies men. Acts 26:18: "Sanctified by faith that is in me." If men live in a way of disobedience they are not Christ's sheep, for His sheep hear His voice (John 10:27). Men that live in a way of disobedience are not born of God. 1 John 3:9: "He that is born of God sinneth not." Men who live in a way of disobedience are the servants of sin. John 8:34: "He that commiteth sin is the servant of sin."

1. A course of external sin is an evidence of hypocrisy, whether it is a sin of omission or commission. If men live in the neglect of known duties or in the practice of known evils, that will be their condem-

nation, let the sin be what it will—let it be profaness, drunkenness, uncleanness, lying, or injustice. Thus it was with the sons of Eli, Hophni and Phineas; they are called "sons of Belial, that knew not the Lord" (1 Samuel 2:12). The foundation of their censure was their profaness and uncleanness (v. 13, 14, 22). So it was with Jehu, notwithstanding his zeal in destroying Baal, because he practiced and tolerated the worship of the calves at Dan and Bethel. 2 Kings 10:31: "Jehu took no heed to walk in the law of the Lord God of Israel, with all his heart and with all his soul; for he turned aside after the sin of Jeroboam." So many of the Pharisees were wicked because they devoured widows' houses (Matthew 23:14). Thus Judas appeared to be a hypocrite because he lived in theft. John 12:6: "He was a thief." That showed the rottenness of the heart of Demas, that he was an apostate. 2 Timothy 4:10: "Demas hath forsaken me, having loved this present evil world." To live impenitently in any outward known sin will cast against a man and prove him an hypocrite.

2. A course of internal sin proves a man to be an hypocrite. Though he washes his hands, if he does not cleanse his heart he is ungodly. The external conversation of some hypocrites may exceed the conversation of some saints; but if there is a way of internal sin their pretenses to godliness are vain. There are two sorts of internal sins which men may live in a way of, and is a witness against them. One is a way of corrupt thoughts and affections. If men allow themselves in malice, envy, wanton or profane thoughts, that will condemn them.

Though those corruptions do not break out in any scandalous way, those thoughts are an evidence of a rotten heart. Titus 3:3: "We ourselves were sometimes foolish, disobedient, deceived, serving divers lusts and pleasures, living in malice and enmity, hateful and hating one another." If a man allows himself, though he thinks he does not, in malice or envy, he is a hypocrite; though his conscience disallows it, yet if his heart allows it he is no saint. If he does not hate and mortify those corrupt affections, he is no saint. The other way of living in internal sin is to live in the omission of spiritual duties. Whether a man knows it or knows it not, it is an evidence of hypocrisy. Many men who make a fair show do not believe in Jesus Christ. They have a persuasion of the truth of the gospel; they hope Christ will save them; they have had some joy in hearing the gospel; but they do not believe in Christ: either they are carnally confident or discouraged. This condemns them. "He that believeth not, the wrath of God abideth on him" (John 3:36). He who is contentious and obeys not the gospel will be condemned (Romans 2:8). So if a man lives in the neglect of love to God, if there is no hearty love to God in his profession, in his obedience, he is not godly. Though there is affection, yet if there is not hearty love, that will condemn him. That was the condemnation of the Jews in John 5:42: "I know you, that you have not the love of God in you." If men are zealous men, if men have tenderness of conscience, if men delight in Sabbaths, but are destitute of love to God, they are hypocrites. So also if there is not a spirit of love to saints. 1 Corinthians 13:1: "If I speak with the tongues of men and angels, and have not charity, I am become as sounding brass, and a tinkling cymbal." So 1 John 4:8: "He that loveth not, knoweth not God."

PROPOSITION 2: Sincerity is known by particular

acts of grace.

The habits of grace cannot be seen immediately. As no man can see his own soul, or any of the faculties of it immediately, so he cannot see the gracious principles that are there immediately. And there is no external act of obedience that is evidential, for an ungodly man may do an external act of obedience. He may give all his goods to the poor and his body to be burned, though he has no charity (1 Corinthians 13:3). But by particular acts of grace they may know their uprightness, and by them only. If a man were to try his sincerity by his certain knowledge of his gracious carriages day by day, he would never attain assurance, but be under perpetual uncertainty. But by particular acts of grace he may know it. Consider:

1. Saints may certainly see particular acts of grace. Though there are many acts of grace that a man does not know to be such, yet some acts of grace are plain to see. We find Christ inquiring of one whether he believed. John 9:35: "Dost thou believe on the Son of God?" And of another whether he loved Him. John 21:16: "Simon, son of Jonas, lovest thou Me?" That shows that such things may be known, else to what purpose would it be to ask those questions? And reason shows that they may be seen, for they greatly differ from all counterfeit acts; and sometimes grace acts very strongly and apparently. And we have an account in Scripture of saints who have spoken very confidently about the workings of a spirit of grace. Job 42:5–6: "Now mine eye seeth Thee, wherefore I abhor myself in dust and ashes." He saw the mighty workings of a spirit of repentance, and was at no loss about it. So David in Psalm 116:1: "I love the Lord." He speaks of it as of a

thing he was assured of. The like workings of heart he found towards the law in Psalm 119:97: "O how I love Thy law." So Peter appeals to Christ, who knew his heart, in John 21:17: "Lord, Thou knowest all things, Thou knowest that I love Thee." And others have had the like experience.

2. Ordinarily they certainly see but few particular acts of grace. There is a very great difference in godly men upon this account. I take it for granted that there are not two men in ten thousand who have just the same experience. More generally, godly men hope and think that they exercise grace many times every day in their prayers, in their callings, and in their conversation with men. But it is but now and then that they can certainly speak up to it. There are great mixtures of corruption with grace; there are many false appearances of grace which make them afraid whether they indeed exercised grace. And this makes it evident that it is thus with saints, that many of them are for a long time under doubts whether they are indeed godly. Thence we have these precepts: 2 Peter 1:10: "Give all diligence to make your calling and election sure." 2 Corinthians 13:5: "Examine yourselves, whether you be in the faith." Some hypocrites are a great deal more confident than many saints. Many godly men are at a loss whether their faith is anything other than what unconverted men may have. And so they are about their other graces; there are some saints who have assurance, but the foundation of it is that now and then they see the plain actings of faith, love, and repentance. They see something of encouragement from their daily walk. But that which begets assurance is that sometimes they plainly see grace.

3. By these visible actings of grace, they may conclude there is a course of gracious carriages. Godly men are described to be men who walk in a course of holiness. Psalm 119:1: "Blessed are the undefiled in the way, that walk in the law of the Lord." And we find that godly men have been well satisfied that they have walked in a way of holiness. 2 Kings 20:3: "Remember, O Lord, I beseech Thee, how I have walked before Thee in truth, and with a perfect heart, and have done that which is good in Thy sight." If it is inquired how they know that their obedience is not the fruit of natural conscience and common grace, as it is with many others, the answer is that they see now and then the plain exercises of grace, and from thence conclude that they are under the influence of a gracious spirit in their walk; that though they are guilty of much formality and hypocrisy, yet there is a spirit of holiness working in them, and a hearty care to keep the commandments of God. If a man sees now and then a spirit of love to God, he may safely conclude that his religion is not the fruit of ostentation or slavish fear, but that a gracious spirit stirs him up to perform his duty, and that his walk is holy.

USE 1. Of awakening to those who live in a course of sin.

Some make pretences to godliness whereby they not only deceive others, but, which is a great deal worse, they deceive themselves also. But this will condemn them: that they live in a course of sin; and such must go with ungodly men. Psalm 125:5: "As for such as turn aside unto their crooked ways, the Lord will lead them forth with the workers of iniquity." If there is a great change in a man's carriage, and he is reformed in several particulars, yet if there is one evil way, the man is an ungodly man. If he does choice service for the church of God, yet he is an ungodly man. Where there is piety, there is universal obedience. A man may have great infirmities, yet be a godly man—so it was with Lot and David and Peter—but if he lives in a way of sin, he does not render his godliness only suspicious, but it is full evidence against him. Men who are godly have a respect to all God's commandments (Psalm 119:1). There are a great many commands, and, if there is one of them that a man has not a respect unto, he will be put to shame another day. If a man lives in one evil way, he is not subject to God's authority; but he then lives in rebellion, and that will take off all his pleas and at once cut off all his pretences, and he will be condemned in the day of judgment. Luke 13:27: "Depart from Me, all ye that work iniquity." One way of sin is exception enough against the man's salvation.

1. Even though the sin that he lives in is small. Such persons will not be guilty of perjury, stealing, drunkenness, or fornication. They look upon them to be heinous things, and they are afraid of them, but they do not much matter if they oppress a little in a bargain, if they commend a thing too much which they are about to sell, if they break a promise, if they spend the Sabbath unprofitably, if they neglect secret prayer, if they talk rudely, and reproach others. They think these things are but small things. If they can keep clear of great transgressions, they hope that God will not insist upon small things; but indeed all the commands of God are established by divine authority, and the man who does not lay weight upon little commands keeps

none as he ought to do. A small bullet may kill a man as well as a cannon ball. A small leak may sink a ship. If a man lives in small sins, that shows that he has no love to God, no sincere care to please and honor God. Little sins are of a damning nature as well as great. If they do not deserve as much punishment as greater, yet they do deserve damnation. There is contempt of God in small sins. Matthew 5:19: "He that shall break one of the lest of these commandments, and shall teach men so, shall be called the least in the kingdom of God." There is rebellion in little sins. Proverbs 19:16: "He that keepeth the commandment keepeth his own soul, but he that despiseth his ways shall die." If a man says, "This is a great command," and so lays weight on it, and another is a little commandment, and so does not regard it, but allows himself to break it, he is in a perishing condition.

2. Even though their temptations are great. Some persons delight in iniquity: they take pleasure in rudeness and intemperate practices. But there are others who do not delight in sin. They can handsomely avoid it, and they do not choose it. Unless they are under some great necessity they will not do it. They are afraid to sin; they think it is dangerous, and have some care to avoid it. But sometimes they force themselves to sin. They are reduced to difficulties, and cannot tell how well to avoid it. It is a dangerous thing not to do it. If Naaman does not bow himself in the house of Rimmon, the king will be in a rage with him, take away his office, and, it may be, take away his life, and so he complies. 2 Kings 5:18: "In this thing the Lord pardon thy servant, that when my master goeth into the house of Rimmon to worship there, and he leaneth on my

hand, and I bow myself in the house of Rimmon, the Lord pardon thy servant in this." So Jeroboam forced himself to set up the calves at Dan and Bethel. He thought if the people went up to Jerusalem to worship, they would return to Rehoboam and kill him. Therefore he must think of some expedient to deliver himself in this strait. 1 Kings 12:28: "Whereupon the king took council, and made two calves of gold; and said to them, 'It is too much for you to go up to Jerusalem, behold thy gods O Israel, which brought thee up out of the land of Egypt.' " He was driven by appearing necessity to take this wicked course. So the stony ground hearers were willing to retain the profession of the true religion, but the case was such that they thought they could not well do it. Matthew 13:21: "When tribulation or persecution ariseth because of the word, by and by he is offended." They would have chosen to have lived and died in the profession of the truth, but they cannot brook confiscation, prisons, and death. And so they must be excused if they drop their profession. So Achan and Gehazi had singular opportunities to get an estate; if they live twenty years, they are not likely to have such an advantage, and they force themselves to borrow a point and break the law of God. They lay a necessity on estate, liberty, and life, but not upon obedience. If a man is willing to serve God in ordinary cases, but excuses himself when there are great difficulties, he is not godly. It is a small matter to serve God when men have no temptation; but Lot was holy in Sodom and Noah was righteous in the old world. Temptations try men, but they do not force men to sin; and grace will establish the heart in a day of temptation. They are blessed who endure temptation (James

1:12). But they are cursed who fall away in a day of temptation.

3. Even though they are afterwards sorry for it. Some men fall into great transgression, but when they consider it they are sorry for it. They do not justify themselves, neither do they excuse themselves, and say others do so as well as they. And if men are left of God who can help it, but they confess it and bewail it before God, it is an affliction to them that they were carried away with temptation. They see they have acted foolishly, that they have despised the commandments of God, and they hope they shall never do so again, be drunk or lie again. Sometimes men take occasion to talk with them, and they are ready to own their fault; they are ashamed, and they shed tears, but after a while the temptation returns and they are as bad as before. They are like the dead fish that are carried down the stream, but they are sorry again, and so they keep on sinning and repenting. Just thus it was with Saul: Jonathan talked to him and he hearkened. 1 Samuel 19:6: "Saul hearkened to Jonathan, and Saul sware, 'As the Lord liveth, he shall not be slain.' " After awhile he was persecuting David again; but upon David's saving his life he wept and made confession. 1 Samuel 24:16: "Saul lifted up his voice and wept." But upon the invitation of the Ziphites he pursued David again, and David spared his life a second time; and upon that Saul confessed and promised. 1 Samuel 26:21: "Then said Saul, 'I have sinned, return my son David, for I will no more do thee harm, I have played the fool, and erred exceedingly.' " There is no trusting such men; if they live in ways of sin, they are ungodly. Godly sorrow will make men live holy lives. 2 Corinthians 7:10: "Godly sorrow worketh

repentance unto salvation, not to be repented of."

USE 2. Encouragement to those who have seen gracious actings in their own hearts.

I suppose that there are several of you who have seen the actings of grace in your own hearts. You have seen the workings of faith, as Paul did in 2 Timothy 1:12: "I know Him whom I have believed"; of love, as Peter in John 21:17: "Lord, Thou knowest all things, Thou knowest that I love Thee"; of repentance, as Job in Job 42:6: "I abhor myself and repent in dust and ashes." You may conclude from hence that you are godly. You may have scruples upon many accounts. You may be under difficulties because God hides His face at present from you. You may have temptation from singular afflictions, or because God denies to answer some prayers in things that lie much upon your hearts. You may have difficulties from such workings of corruption as seems to be inconsistent with grace. You may have temptation because you do not seem to grow; but if you have certainly seen the working of a gracious spirit, if a hundred times, if ten times, or if one time, you may conclude that you are godly. That which was not in being could not be seen; that which is not, is invisible. If there were no sun, moon, or stars, none could be seen. So, if there were no faith or love, they could not be seen. There may be grace where it is not seen; but, where it is seen, there it is. And you may conclude that you are godly. For:

1. This shows that there was at the time a principle of grace. The habits of grace are not immediately to be seen but only by their workings. If there is a gracious act, there must be a gracious principle. If there is not

an antecedent one, there must be at least a concomitant one; for while a man remains in his natural condition he cannot act graciously. Romans 8:7: "The natural mind is enmity to God, and is not subject to the law of God, neither indeed can be." If a man loves God, he is disposed to love Him; if he believes in Christ, he is disposed to believe in Christ. It is impossible to do those actions without a disposition to them; and that disposition is a principle or habit of grace.

Every man who acts graciously is a new creature. Until the heart is changed, it will not carry graciously. Any act of grace is a sure token of regeneration. If a man believes in Christ, he is certainly born of God. John 1:12–13: "To them that received Him gave He power to become the sons of God, even to them that believe on His name, who were born not of blood, nor of the will of the flesh, nor of the will of man, but of God." If a man breathes, sees, hears, and walks, he is certainly a living man. Where there is an act of life, there is a principle of life. 1 John 3:7: "He that doth righteousness is righteous, as He is righteous."

Every effect must have a proper cause. If the heart were utterly opposed to believing, loving, or repenting, he would not believe, love, or repent. The heart of a man is always inclined to what he chooses. The mind may understand a thing that it is not inclined to understand; but the will never chooses without an inclination so to do. If there is a change in the behavior of the heart, there is a change in the disposition of the heart.

2. If a principle of grace was once there, it is always there. It was otherwise under the covenant of works. Adam's grace was perfect, but mutable; for he did not fulfill the condition of the covenant. If he had once

done that, his grace would have been immutable. But under the new covenant, if a man is once godly, he always will be godly; for everyone who is godly has fulfilled the condition of the covenant. Grace may decay, but it never will be lost. It may wither, but never die. Common grace may be lost, but saving grace cannot be lost. If grace is once begun it will continue. Philippians 1:6: "I am confident of this very thing, that He that hath begun a good work in you, will perfect it to the day of Christ." The power of God is engaged for the preservation of grace, so once godly always godly. 1 Peter 1:5: "Who are kept by the power of God, through faith unto salvation." Sometimes they are afraid they shall fall away, but whether they have more strength or less strength they shall never fall away. God's covenant is their security.

Such men may have great temptations. Heretics may endeavor to seduce them, vicious men may seek to debauch them, worldly men may entice them, and persecutors may seek to frighten them out of their religion—but nothing can be too hard for them. "Many waters cannot quench love, neither can the floods drown it" (Song of Solomon 8:7). They may have temptation to pride, to presumption, or to discouragement, but if they are led into temptation, they will be delivered from evil.

A principle of grace is like a living fountain. John 4:14: "Whosoever drinketh of the water that I shall give him, shall never thirst; but the water that I shall give him, shall be in him a well of water springing up into everlasting life." False-hearted men may fall away, but those who are sincere will be more than conquerors. If Abraham is once godly, he will continue so, though he lives a hundred and seventy years. If grace is begun here, it will be perfected in heaven.

USE 3. Of direction to godly men, how you may know your sincerity, which is by renewing the visible actings of grace.

Many signs are given of holiness that will not bear examination, and there is danger that many are deceived thereby. Some godly, and some ungodly men, who find them in themselves, may be comforted thereby, but they beget no assurance. And some men who find them in themselves remain at a loss whether they are godly or not. The way to know your godliness is to renew the visible exercises of grace. When a man sees that he loves God and believes in Jesus Christ, he will not be unsatisfied about his godliness. If he has been in the dark, and in great temptations just before, yet this will beget assurance.

Here you may observe:

1. If you do not know that you live in sin, that can be no evidence of your godliness. As you cannot condemn yourselves, so you cannot justify yourselves. Some persons examine themselves whether they live in any known sin; and upon the strictest enquiry they do not find that they do. They do not find that they live in the neglect of any duty, or in the commission of any sin. Their hearts do not reproach them. They duly attend prayer; they are careful to sanctify the Sabbath; they live soberly, chastely, and justly; they are true to their word and faithful in their places; they do not know upon the most narrow search that they live in any way of sin, yet they cannot justify themselves from hence. 1 Corinthians 4:4: "I know nothing of myself, yet am I not hereby

justified." For men who examine themselves may be ignorant that they live in a way of sin, yet they may live in a way of sin. Men's understandings are corrupted, and they may live in pride, worldliness and unbelief, and not know it. They may think those corruptions do not reign when indeed they do reign. Many men who do not know that they live in sin are fain to suspend their judgment about themselves; they hope from hence that they are holy, but do not know it. Though men do not know that they live in sin, yet God may know that they do. Proverbs 30:12: "There is a generation that is pure in their own eyes, yet are not cleansed from their filthiness."

2. If there is a great probability that you live in a way of faith, love, and repentance, that does not make it evident. There is some probability of some men's faith because gospel promises have been a comfort to them; of their love, because they are zealous and delight in ordinances, and in praising God; of their repentance, for their sins are a great burden to them, and they are careful to avoid sin. But probabilities prove nothing. That may be probable that may be false; there may be some probability of a thing, yet the contrary may be certain. Probabilities leave men under uncertainties. If they raise hopes, yet they leave room for fears. There may be probabilities one way and as great probabilities the other way. Men will not content themselves with a probable title to their land. God will not take men to heaven because there is a probability of their goodness. Twenty probabilities make the thing more probable, but they do not make it certain. Probabilities are not demonstration. The hopes that are built on them may be disappointed. Therefore we are directed to "make

our calling and election sure" (2 Peter 1:10).

3. All the visible exercises of grace are evidential. The Word of God tells that all who believe in Jesus Christ are children of God. John 1:12: "To them that receive Him, gave He power to become the sons of God." It tells that all who love God are heirs of heaven. James 1:12: "God has promised a crown of life to them that love Him." It tells us that all who have godly sorrow shall be saved. 2 Corinthians 7:10: "Godly sorrows worketh repentance unto salvation." It tells us that all who love the brethren shall have eternal life. 1 John 3:14: "We know that we are translated from death to life, because we love the brethren." Hence, if any of these workings are clearly seen, the man has a sure evidence of his good estate. He has ground to cast the case for himself. It is no presumption for him to conclude his justification. He has a divine warrant to give sentence for himself. At such a time when he pronounces himself a saint, he goes according to law and evidence. His confidence is assurance, for those exercises of grace that he is conscious of are peculiar to godly men, and assuredly distinguish them from all other men.

4. The more these visible exercises of grace are renewed, the more certain you will be; the more frequently these actings are renewed, the more abiding and confirmed your assurance will be. A man who has been assured of such visible exercises of grace may quickly afterwards be in doubt whether he was not mistaken; but when such actings are renewed again and again, he grows more settled and established about his good estate. If a man sees a thing once, that makes him sure; but if afterwards he fears he was deceived when he comes to see it again, he is more sure he is not mis-

taken. If a man reads such passages in a book, he is sure it is so. Some months afterwards some may bear him down that he was mistaken, so as to make him question it himself; but when he looks and reads it again he is abundantly confirmed. The more men's grace is multiplied, the more their peace is multiplied. 2 Peter 1:2: "Grace and peace be multiplied unto you through the knowledge of God and Jesus our Lord." The third time the question was put to Peter whether he loved Christ, he answered with greater assurance. The very proposing of the question stirred up the working of a spirit of love, and he spoke with very great confidence (John 21:16–17). The first and second time he said, "Yea, Lord, Thou knowest that I love Thee." But the third time he spoke with greatest assurance, "Lord, Thou knowest all things, Thou knowest that I love Thee." It went greatly to his heart that his love should be so often questioned, and so he was more abundantly satisfied in the truth of his love.

The Defects of Preachers Reproved

"The scribes and the Pharisees sit in Moses' seat.
All therefore whatsoever they bid you observe,
that observe and do." Matthew 23:2–3

In these words is a direction given by Christ unto
the people, where we have:

First, the foundation of the rule: "the scribes and
Pharisees sit in Moses' seat." Some take this as spoken
of the Sanhedrin, who were the successors of Moses
and the seventy elders of Israel. Possibly that may be a
mistake, for several of the Sanhedrin were not Pharisees (Acts 23:3). For the chief priests belonged to that
society (Acts 4:6), and they are said to be Sadducees; but
by scribes and Pharisees I understand the principal
teachers among the Jews. The priests and Levites were
more especially devoted to the study of the law.
Deuteronomy 33:10: "They shall teach Jacob Thy judgments, and Israel Thy law." Yet others who were learned
in the law were made use of to instruct the people, and
were chosen to be rulers of the synagogues. The
Pharisees were of any tribe. Paul, who was of the tribe of
Benjamin, was a Pharisee by education, as he tells in
Acts 23:6: "I am a Pharisee, the son of a Pharisee."

Second, here is the rule given: "what they bid you
observe, that observe and do." This must be understood
with the limitation: when they teach according to the
mind of God. Sometimes they taught for doctrines the

commandments of men and then it was sinful and
dangerous to observe their directions. "If the blind lead
the blind, both shall fall into the ditch" (Matthew
15:14).

**DOCTRINE: There may be a great deal of good
preaching in a country, and yet a great want of good
preaching.**

It is a felicity to a people when there is good preaching in the land, yet there may in the same land be great
want of good teaching. Some things that are very useful
may be plainly and fully taught, and other things that
might be as useful may be neglected. Many sound principles in religion may be taught, and other things that
are of great concern unto souls may be omitted.
Ministers don't sufficiently do their duty if they preach
many sound truths, and do it convincingly and with
good affection, if they do it with great clearness and evidence, provided they neglect other things that are
needful to salvation. And so it falls out sometimes that
men who make many good sermons are very defective
in preaching some other things that they ought to
preach.

I shall clear this in three instances.

1. The scribes and Pharisees in Israel taught the
people that there was only one God, the Maker of all
things, and were great enemies to the idolatry that
their fathers were guilty of before the Babylonian captivity. As the scribe said to Christ in Mark 12:32, "Well,
Master, Thou hast said the truth: for there is one God,
and there is none other but He." They taught many
moral duties: that men must love God and believe His
Word, that they must be just and chaste and men of
truth, and were very strict in the observation of the

Sabbath. They limited men how far they might go on the Sabbath (Acts 1:12). We read of "a Sabbath day's journey." They taught truly the doctrine of the resurrection of the dead (Acts 23:7–8). The Pharisees dissented from the Sadducees. The Sadducees say there is no resurrection, nor angel, nor spirit, but the Pharisees confessed both. They taught that the Messiah was to come; the Samaritans themselves received that doctrine (John 4:25). They were very punctual in teaching circumcision and the ceremonies of the law of Moses, about sacrifices, tithes, and legal uncleanness. But they were very faulty in preaching in other particulars. They were ignorant of the doctrine of regeneration, so Nicodemus (John 3:4) says, "How can a man be born when he is old?" They taught that the first motions of lust, if the will did not consent, were not sins. As we may gather from Romans 7:7, Paul says, "I had not known lust, except the Law had said, 'Thou shall not covet.' " And from Matthew 5:27–28, "It was said by them of old time, 'Thou shalt not commit adultery.' But I say whosoever looketh on a woman to lust after her hath committed adultery in his heart."

They taught also that dangerous doctrine of justification by works (Romans 10:3). They went about to establish their own righteousness (Romans 9:2–3). They sought it, as it were, by the works of the law. They taught the people that in case they devoted their estates to the temple, they need not relieve their fathers or mothers (Matthew 15:4–6). And above all they taught that Jesus of Nazareth was not the Messiah and brought many objections against Him. They said that He came out of Galilee, was a gluttonous man and a wine-bibber (Matthew 11:19), a friend of publicans and sinners.

They reproached Him that by the devil He cast out devils, and they were very dull in their preaching (Matthew 7:29).

2. The papists teach the doctrine of the Trinity truly, and the attributes of God, so also the doctrine of the Incarnation of Christ, and that He died for our redemption and is at the right hand of God. They teach the doctrine of the day of judgment, of heaven and of hell, and many moral rules. But they preach a multitude of false doctrines with these doctrines that are pernicious to the souls of men. They teach men to seek the pardon of their sin by afflicting their bodies, by pilgrimage and paying a sum of money. They teach many horrible things with respect to their Pope, that he has power to forgive sin, to dispense with incestuous marriages; that he has power over all the churches and may dispense with the laws of God; that he is infallible. They teach the doctrine of image worship, abolishing the second commandment. They teach prayer to saints departed, the unlawfulness of priests' marriages, the doctrine of purgatory, justification by works, a conditional election, the power of free will, falling from grace, and hundreds of other erroneous doctrines. They indeed subvert the faith of Christ.

3. Many Arminians preach very profitably about God and the person of Christ, about justification by faith and universal obedience, about the day of judgment and of eternal rewards and punishments. But there is a great deal of want of good preaching among them. They decry all absolute decrees of election and reprobation, making the decrees of God to depend on the foresight of repentance or impenitence. They assert universal redemption, as if Christ died to make all man save-

able. They deny the propagation of sin, saying men become sinners by imitation. They hold a power in man to withstand the grace of God; that after God has done His work it is in the power of man to refuse to be converted. They don't acknowledge the servitude of man to sin, but have power with that assistance that God affords to convert himself. They deny the doctrine of perseverance. These things draw a great train of errors after them.

The reason of the doctrine is because some preachers are men of learning and moral men, and they have drunk in some errors and lack experience. Learning and morality will qualify men to make many good and profitable sermons, much for the edification of the hearers. Learning qualifies men to clear up many principles of religion, and a moral disposition may fit men zealously to reprove vicious practices. But men may be learned men, yet drink in very corrupt doctrines.

Learning is no security against erroneous principles. The Pharisees and Sadducees were men of liberal education, yet leavened with many false principles. Matthew 16:6: "Beware of the leaven of the Pharisees and Sadducees." And verse 12: "Then understood they that He bid them not beware of the leaven of bread, but of the doctrine of the Pharisees and of the Sadducees." Learning will not cure those distempers of the heart that expose men to false opinions. Learning will not cure the pride and conceitedness of men's hearts. Men of learning may lean too much to their own understanding. Men of learning may be led aside by reading erroneous books. A learned education will not deliver men from carnal reason. Men of corrupt affections are very inclined to imbibe bad principles. Men of learning may be blind men. Christ says of the Pharisees, "They be blind leaders of the blind" (Matthew 15:14).

Most of the errors in the world in matters of religion have been hatched by men of learning. Arius, Socinus, Arminius, and Pelagius were learned men. Errors in religion have been generally the offspring of great scholars, and have been propagated by them. And men may be moral men who have no experience of the work of God upon their hearts. Men may be zealous men against drunkenness and whoredom who have no saving knowledge of Christ. Many moral men have no communion with God, no experience of a saving change in their own souls. Men may be very moral and have no experience of a work of humiliation or being brought off from their own righteousness, or a work of faith; of the difference that is between the common and special work of the Spirit; of the difference between saving and common illumination; of the working of the heart under temptation; of the way wherein godly men are wont to find relief.

Every learned and moral man is not a sincere convert, and so not able to speak exactly and experimentally to such things as souls want to be instructed in. It is as with a man who has seen a map of a country, or has read a great deal about it: he can't tell the way between town and town, and hundreds of particular circumstances, as a man who has traveled or lived there is able to do. Experience fits men to teach others. A man who has himself had only a common work of the Spirit, and judges it saving, is very unfit to judge the state of other men. Men would not put their lives into the hands of an unskillful physician, or trust their ship with an unskillful pilot, or an intricate case depending on the law with an unskillful lawyer.

USE 1. Of examination whether it is not thus in this country.

It is notoriously known by those who are acquainted with the state of the Christian world that though there are many eminent truths taught, yet there is a great want of good preaching. Whence it comes to pass that among professors a spirit of piety runs exceedingly low. But it is proper for us to take notice how it is among ourselves; and though it is very evident that there is a great deal of good preaching in the land, that the way of salvation is preached with a great deal of plainness and power, and many men are very faithful to declare all the counsel of God, yet there may be cause of lamentation that there is a great deal wanting in some places. Some may be very much to blame in preaching as they ought to do.

If any are taught that frequently men are ignorant of the time of their conversion, that is not good preaching. Some are of that opinion, and it is likely they may drink it in from their ministers. This is a delusion, and it may do them a great deal of hurt; it hardens men in their natural condition. Paul knew the time of his conversion: "At midday, O King, I saw a light from heaven, above the brightness of the sun" (Acts 26:13).

Men are frequently at a loss whether their conversion was true or not; but surely men who are converted must take some notice of the time when God made a change in them. Conversion is a great change, from darkness to light, from death to life, from the borders of despair to a spirit of faith in Christ. As for the outward conversation, there is sometimes little difference.

Men might carry very well before, but, as to the frame of men's hearts, there is a very great difference. Formerly they were under the reigning power of objections against the gospel; when converted they receive it as a divine truth. Before they were converted they were under a sentence of condemnation; now they have peace with God through Jesus Christ. Men are generally a long time seeking conversion, laboring to get an interest in Christ; and it would be much if when God reveals Christ to them they should not take notice of it when the change is made. Ten to one but conscience will take notice of it.

When a seaman comes into the harbor, when a prisoner is pardoned, when a victory is obtained, when a disease is broken, it would be much if men should take no notice of them. Conversion is the greatest change that men undergo in this world; surely it falls under observation! The prodigal knew well enough the time of his return to his father's house. The children of Israel knew the time of their passing over Jordan.

If any are taught that humiliation is not necessary before faith, that is not good preaching. Such doctrine has been taught privately and publicly, and is a means to make some men mistake their condition and think themselves happy when they are miserable. For men must be brought off from their own righteousness before they are brought to Christ. Men who think they have anything to appease the wrath of God and ingratiate themselves will not accept the calls of the gospel in sincerity. While people have a foundation to build upon, they will not build upon Christ. A self-righteous spirit is quite contrary to the gospel. If men are self-righteous men, they will not judge it fair for God to cast them off. Men who depend upon the justice of God will not depend upon the mere mercy of God. Men who lay claim to heaven from their own works will not depend on the plea that Christ has given His life a ransom for many, and has redeemed us from the curse, being made a curse for us.

Multitudes of men are ruined by building upon a sandy foundation. Men must see their malady before they see their remedy. Men must be led into understanding of the badness of their hearts and the strictness of the law before they will be convinced of the preciousness of Christ. Men who can heal their own consciences will not come to Christ for healing. Men must be driven by necessity indeed before they come to Christ. Though men feel great terrors and live a tormented life, yet they will not come to Christ until driven out of themselves. Men must feel themselves dead in sin in order to their believing. Romans 7:9: "Sin revived, and I died." Men must see themselves poor and miserable, wretched and blind and naked, before they receive that counsel of buying of Christ gold tried in the fire, and white raiment (Revelation 3:17).

When men don't preach much about the danger of damnation, there is a want of good preaching. Some ministers preach much about moral duties and the blessed estate of godly men, but don't seek to awaken sinners and make them sensible of their danger; they cry for reformation. These things are very needful in their places to be spoken unto, but if sinners don't hear often of judgment and damnation, few will be converted. Many men are in a deep sleep and flatter themselves as if there was no hell, or at least that God will not deal so harshly with them as to damn them. Psalm 36:2: "He flattereth himself in his own eyes, until his iniquity be found to be hateful."

Men need to be told of the terrors of the Lord so that they may flee from wrath to come. A little matter will not scare men. Their hearts are as hard as a stone, as hard as a piece of nether millstone, and they will be ready to laugh at the shaking of the spear. Ministers must give them no rest in such a condition. They must pull themselves as brands out of the burnings. It is well if thunder and lightning will awaken them. They need to fear that they may work out their salvation with fear and trembling. Ministers are faulty when they speak to them with gentleness, as Eli rebuked his sons. Christ Jesus often warned them of the danger of damnation. Matthew 5:29–30: "It is better that one of thy members should perish, and not that the whole body should be cast into hell." Matthew 7:13: "Broad is the gate and wide is the way that leadeth to destruction, and many there be that go in thereat." Matthew 13:42: "The angels shall cast them into a furnace of fire, there shall be wailing and gnashing of teeth." (See also Matthew 22:13 and 25:41, 46.) This is for our imitation.

Christ knew how to deal with souls, and Paul followed His example. Men need to be terrified and have the arrows of the Almighty in them that they may be converted. Ministers should be sons of thunder. Men need to have storms in their hearts before they will betake themselves to Christ for refuge. When they are pricked at the heart, then they will say, "What must we do to be saved?" Men must be fired out of their worldliness and sloth. Men must be driven as Lot was out of Sodom. Reason will govern men in other things, but it is fear that must make them diligently seek salvation. If they are but thoroughly convinced of their danger, that will make them go to God and take pains.

If they give a wrong account of the nature of justifying faith, that is not good preaching. Justifying faith is set forth in the Scripture by many figurative expressions: coming to Christ, opening to Him, sitting under His shadow, flying to Him for refuge, building on Him as on a foundation, feeding on Him. These expressions imply not only an act of the understanding, but also an act of the will, accepting Him, depending on Him. This doctrine is despised by some, and faith in Christ is said to be only a persuasion of the truth of the Christian religion. This is the way to make multitudes of carnal men secure, and to flatter themselves as if they were in a good condition. They say they are not heathens, Turks, papists, or Jews. Since they believe that Jesus Christ is the eternal Son of God, they hope they are believers; but multitudes of people have such a faith that will fall short of eternal life. John 2:23–24: "Many believed in His name, when they saw the miracles that He did; but Jesus did not commit Himself unto them." John 12:42: "Among the chief rulers many believed on Him, but because of the Pharisees they did not confess Him."

The faith of some men is only a persuasion from their education. As heathens receive the religion of their forefathers by tradition, so these receive the Christian religion from hearsay. But justifying faith is wrought in men by the mighty power of God. 2 Thessalonians 1:11: "That He would work in you the work of faith with power." Ephesians 1:19–20: "And what is the exceeding greatness of His power to us who believe, according to the working of His mighty power; which He wrought in Christ when He raised Him from the dead." By justifying faith, men answer the calls of God, relinquishing their own righteousness; they place their dependence only on the mediation of Christ (Hebrews 6:18). They flee for refuge, to lay hold on the hope that is set before them. Justifying faith is a living principle that sanctifies men. Acts 15:9: "Purifying their hearts by faith." Many men have a common persuasion of the truth of the gospel who are utterly destitute of holiness. But true justifying faith is always accompanied with a holy life. Where there is faith, there is every other grace. Acts 26:18: "Sanctified by faith that is in me."

If any give false signs of godliness, that is not good preaching. Signs of grace are of two sorts. Some are probable, and they must be spoken of only as probable; a score of them may make the thing more probable, but don't make it certain. Probabilities make no demonstration. Probable signs are not conclusive. There are two errors in laying down signs. One is when those things that may flow from common principles—such as natural temper, natural conscience, fear of hell, or false imaginations—are given as sure signs of grace. But those things that may flow from common principles don't truly distinguish between saints and hypocrites, things such as a good conversation, savory discourse, zeal against sin, strong religious affections, sorrow for sin, quietness under afflictions, delight in ordinances, or suffering for religion. From such loose signs people are in danger of taking up a false persuasion of their godliness.

Such signs are full of delusion, and many men bless themselves who are in a miserable condition. Such probable signs may be where there are certain signs of the contrary. Men are apt to flatter themselves, and when they hear such signs they are strengthened in their carnal confidence. There is no infallible sign of grace but grace. Grace is known only by intuition; all the external effects of grace may flow from other causes. Another error is when men are too strict in their signs, as when they give that as a sign that there is a constant care to glorify God, a continual living upon Jesus Christ, and a constant watchfulness against the workings of corruption. There is no godly man but has at times ill frames of spirit. David and Jonah and Peter had such. When David committed adultery, he had not a due care to glorify God; nor Jonah when he was in a fret, nor the Psalmist when he was as a beast before God, nor Paul when he was led into captivity by the law of sin that was in his members. There is no godly man who can comfort himself with such signs as these. It is well if godly men see now and then the workings of a spirit of grace. Grace is many times under hatches and is invisible.

If any teach men to build their faith about the divine authority of the Scripture upon probable signs, that is not good preaching. There are many probable arguments for the authority of the sacred Scriptures: the eminency of the penmen, and they have had a mighty efficacy to make a change in the hearts of men. It is said there were many miracles wrought for the confirmation of the doctrine of them; there has been an accomplishment of many of the predictions in them. These arguments are preponderating and outweigh all objections that are brought against the authority of them. These considerations may well strengthen the faith of the people of God, but these things cannot be the foundation of our faith. It is only the certain knowledge of their authority that can be the foundation of faith or any other grace. Men cannot believe them to be infallibly true upon probable arguments. Probable arguments must be looked on but as probable and not convincing. Men must have infallible arguments for loving God and believing His Word. The foundation of believing the divine authority of the Scripture is the manifestation of the divine glory in them. There is a self-evidencing light in the works of God. The creation of the world shows God's power and the Godhead (Romans 1:20). It is impossible that the world should be made by any but an infinite God. So there is a self-evidencing light in the Word of God; there are such things revealed there as can be made known by none but God. 1 Corinthians 2:9: "Eye hath not seen, nor ear heard, nor hath it entered into the heart of man to conceive what God hath prepared for them that love Him." Those eternal rewards that are spoken of in the Scripture, those perfect rules that are laid down there, those accounts that are given of the mercy of God and the justice of God, manifested in the way of our salvation, would never have entered into the heart of man to conceive if it had not been revealed by God. Men would never have thought of such a way of salvation if it had not been declared by God.

If men preach for such liberties as God does not allow, that is not good preaching. There are many licentious liberties that are taken by men in their apparel, in their drinking, in their dancing and other recreations, in their discourses upon the Sabbath, and in their dealings with one another. And if ministers either vindicate or connive at them, they don't preach as they ought to do. Some men are lax casuists, and they take too great a liberty themselves, as do their wives and children, and they are afraid to anger men by reproving some particular evils that men are addicted to who prevail in the land. The Pharisees were such casuists. Matthew 5:43: "Ye have heard it hath been said of old, 'Thou shalt love thy neighbor, and hate thine enemy.' " Men should be solemnly warned against all evil carriages; and if this is omitted it gives great increase to sin in the land. God complains of ill against teachers for not reproving sinners. Isaiah 56:10: "They are ignorant and blind, dumb dogs that cannot bark." If men were duly reproved for their extravagancies, that would be a means to reclaim them. Jeremiah 23:22: "If they had stood in My counsel and had caused My people to hear My words; then they should have turned them from their evil way and from the evil of their doings."

Faithful preaching would be beneficial two ways: one way is it would cut off occasions of anger and prevent those sins that bring down the wrath of God on the land; we should then enjoy much more public prosperity. The other is, that it would deliver men from those vicious practices that are a great hindrance to conversion. As long as men live in ways of intemperance, injustice, and unsuitable carriages on the Sabbath, it will be a great impediment to a thorough work of conversion. There may be conversion though men are not broken off from sins of ignorance, but as long as they tolerate themselves in immoralities that will be a mighty bar in the way of their conversion.

If men preach for such ceremonies in worship as God does not allow, that is not good preaching. There are those who plead for human inventions in worship, who would if they could defend the ceremonies of the Church of England, who would retain some Jewish ceremonies that are abolished, and practice other human appointments. Jeroboam was condemned not only for worshipping the calves of Dan and Bethel, but for appointing a time of worship in his own heart (1 Kings 12:32–33). So it is noted as an imperfection in the reformation of Asa, Jehoshaphat and Manasseh that the high places were not taken away. This is spoken of as a great sign of hypocrisy. Isaiah 29:13: "This people draw near Me with their mouth, and honor Me with their lips; but have removed their heart far from Me; and their fear towards Me is taught by the precept of men." When men impose such ceremonies, they usurp a power that God has not given them. It is God's prerogative to appoint in what ways we shall worship Him; and men therein go quite beyond the bounds of their authority. Men therein impute imperfection and defect to the ordinances of God, as if they could teach Him how it is fit that He should be worshipped, and they presume on a blessing without a promise. Matthew 15:9: "In vain do they worship Me, teaching for doctrines the commandments of men." This is a way to make men formal in their worship; the multiplying of ceremonies eats out the heart of religion and makes a people degenerate. Men who multiply ceremonies are apt to content themselves with the form without the life.

QUESTION. Is the late practice of some ministers in reading their sermons commendable?

ANSWER. There are some cases wherein it may be tolerable. Persons through age may lose the strength of their memories, and be under a necessity to make use of their notes—but ordinarily it is not to be allowed.

Consideration 1. It was not the manner of the prophets or apostles. Baruch read the roll that was written from the mouth of Jeremiah; but Jeremiah was not wont to read his prophesies. It was the manner of the Jews to read the Scriptures in the synagogues; but after that it was their way to instruct and exhort men, not from any written copy. Acts 13:15: "After the reading of the law and the prophets, the rulers of the synagogue sent to them, saying, 'Men and brethren, if ye have any word of exhortation for the people, say on.' " This was according to the example of Christ (Luke 4:17, 20). It was ordered in England in the days of King Edward the Sixth that ministers should read printed homilies in public. And there was great necessity of it, for there was not one in ten who were able to make sermons. But it has been the manner of worthy men both here and in other places to deliver their sermons without their notes.

Consideration 2. Reading sermons is a dull way of preaching. Sermons when read are not delivered with authority and in an affecting way. It is prophesied of Christ (Micah 5:4): "He shall stand and feed in the strength of the Lord, in the majesty of the name of the Lord His God." When sermons are delivered without notes, the looks and gesture of the minister are a great means to command attention and stir up affection. Men are apt to be drowsy in hearing the Word, and the liveliness of the preacher is a means to stir up the attention of the hearers and beget suitable affection in them. Sermons that are read are not delivered with authority; they favor the sermons of the scribes (Matthew 7:29). Experience shows that sermons read are not so profitable as others. It may be argued that it is harder to remember rhetorical sermons than mere rational discourses; but it may be answered that it is far more profitable to preach in the demonstrations of the Spirit than with the enticing words of man's wisdom.

USE 2. See the reason why there is so little effect of preaching. There is much good preaching, and yet there is want of good preaching. There is very good preaching in old England, yet there is great want of good preaching, especially among the conformists. And there is very good preaching in New England, and yet there is some want of good preaching, especially in some places: and this is one reason that there is no more good done. There is a great fault in hearers: they are not studious of the mind of God; they are enemies to the gospel. And when Christ Himself preached among them many did not profit by it. Yet some preachers are much to blame, and though they preach profitably many times, yet they have great cause to be humbled for their defects.

For hence it is that there is so little conversion. There is great complaint in one country and in another that there are few converted. It is apparent by men's unsanctified lives and their unsavory discourses. This is one reason, there is a great deal of preaching that does not much promote it, but is a hindrance to it. To tell men that they may be converted though they don't know the time; to teach that there is no need of a work of humiliation to prepare them for Christ; and that faith is nothing else but a persuasion that the gospel is true, is the very way to make many carnal men hope that they are converted. It makes other preaching very ineffectual; it makes them think that it is needless to strive for conversion. Such preaching hardens men in their sins. The want of dealing plainly with men is the reason why there is seldom a noise among the dry bones.

In some towns there is no such thing to be observed for twenty years together. And men continue in a senseless condition, come to meetings and hear preaching, but are never the better for it. In some towns godly men are very thinly sown. Most of the people are in as bad a condition as if they had never heard the gospel. They go on in a still way, following their worldly designs, carry on somewhat of the form of godliness, but mind little but the world and the pleasures of this life. The scribes did not preach with authority (Matthew 7:29). They did not enter into the kingdom of God themselves, and they who were entering in they hindered. Such preaching is not mighty to the pulling down of strongholds. Conversion work will fail very much where there is not sound preaching.

Hence many men who make a high profession lead unsanctified lives. They are not dealt plainly with; and so, though they profess high, they live very low. They are not dealt roundly with, and they believe they are in a good estate, and conscience suffers them to live after a corrupt manner. Some of them live a proud and voluptuous life, and they are not searched as they should be. If they were told their own, that would keep them from saying that they were rich and increased in goods, and had need of nothing. If they were rebuked sharply, that might be a means to make them sound in the faith (Titus 1:13). It might make them not only to reform, but lay a better foundation for eternal life than ever yet was laid. Paul was very thorough in his work, and wherever he came he had the fullness of the blessing of the gospel of Christ (Romans 15:29).

The Presence of Christ with the Ministers of the Gospel

A Sermon Preached January 1, 1717
at the Ordination of the Reverend Joseph Willard

"And lo, I am with you always, even unto the end
of the world. Amen." Matthew 28:20

Christ Jesus, in the 18th verse, acquaints the disciples with His own authority: "All power is given unto Me in heaven and in earth." And then He exercises His authority in commissioning them. And, first, He tells them to whom they shall go: to all nations as they had opportunity. They were forbidden formerly to go to the Gentiles. "Go not into the way of the Gentiles and into any city of the Samaritans enter ye not" (Matthew 10:5), but now He takes off that prohibition, though they were first to offer the gospel to the Jews. Paul and Barnabas told the Jews that it was necessary that the gospel should first be spoken to them (Acts 13:46).

Second, here are the several offices which they were to attend: they were to make disciples. We render it "teach," but the word means "disciple all nations." They were to bring them to the acknowledgment of Christ and the profession of the gospel. Also, they were to baptize them in the name of the Father, the Son, and the Holy Ghost. This is a seal of the covenant that succeeds in the place of circumcision, representing our being washed from our sins in the blood of Christ. This must be applied to all disciples, both adults and infants. Then, they must teach them all rules of obedience. This comprehends the whole law of God, both moral and instituted—whatever was their duty to practice, that was the duty of the disciples to preach. This work that He sets them about was attended with much difficulty, considering the corruption of nature, and the prejudices that both Jews and Gentiles were under. Therefore He encouraged them that He will be with them. He would have them take special notice of it: "Lo, I am with you."

Mind here, first, what He promised, that is, His presence. He was about to be removed to heaven, but He tells them that He will be with them. Though He was absent as to His human nature, yet He would be with them by His Spirit and His power. Second, the persons to whom the promise is made, and they are immediately the eleven apostles, but He intends their successors also. They could live but a little while, but He promised His presence to the end of the world.

DOCTRINE: Christ Jesus will be present with the ministers of the gospel to the end of the world.

Christ was eminently with the apostles, so that in a short time they set up churches in many parts of the world and laid a foundation for the profession of the Christian religion, both among civil and barbarous nations; and the ministers in these days must not expect such extraordinary gifts or such wonderful success as they had—yet they have the word of Christ that He will be with them. They may conclude that Satan will be busy to oppose them; but this is their encouragement: that Christ will be present with them. The work of the ministry is difficult work. Paul says, "Who is sufficient for these things?" (2 Corinthians 2:16). But yet there is no reason that they should faint under their burden, for Christ says He will be with them. The ministers of the gospel are Christ's ministers, and their service is service for Christ; therefore it is no wonder that He will be present with them. When God sent Moses to the children of Israel, He told them that He would be with them; and it is a great comfort to the people that Christ will be with their ministers. And this is not the privilege of one generation or a few generations, but of all generations to the end of the world.

Here it is asked: How do ministers need the presence of Christ? And how will Christ be present with them?

QUESTION. How do ministers need the presence of Christ?

ANSWER 1. To furnish them with gifts for their work. There was need of extraordinary gifts in the beginning of the gospel for the removal of prejudices: both Jews and Gentiles, by reason of their education, were under prejudices, and there was need of miraculous gifts to prepare them to consider impartially the doctrine taught by the apostles. And ministers now need Christ's presence to furnish them with gifts; there is need of a great deal of wisdom to find out acceptable words. Ecclesiastes 12:10: "The Preacher sought to find acceptable words."

They need a great deal of knowledge to make them fit for their work. The minister needs great knowledge in the Scripture to enable him to answer all cases of conscience that may be put to him, to help persons who are in the dark to judge aright of their condition, to enable them to see their sincerity or their hypocrisy.

They need a great deal of light from Christ so that they may understand the truth in things that are contro- verted and lead the people in the right way. There is an abundance of mistakes among men in matters of reli- gion. Some of them very dangerous, all are of ill conse- quence; and ministers need light from God so that they may not be blind guides. They need divine teaching that they may be able to convince men who oppose the truth; and to establish them who receive it. He must be able to convince gainsayers (Titus 1:9). There is a great deal of darkness among men about matters of faith, about moral rules, and about divine institutions; and ministers need to be taught of God that they may teach people the good and right way. It is not enough for a minister to be able to make some edifying discourses; he should be able to set those points that are more in- tricate in a true light, and to speak accurately to all those cases that the souls of men need help in.

ANSWER 2. To strengthen them against temptation. The calling of a minister lays him open to great temp- tation, especially through a spirit of fear to neglect his duty. Sometimes he is called to preach such truths as will be offensive to some and stir up their displeasure and opposition; sometimes to give such reproofs as will be taken very hardly by some men, they will not stom- ach it that they are reflected upon; sometimes he is un- der a necessity to deal with some men who don't know how to bear it. And there is danger of being out-bid with a spirit of fear. Some are his friends and he is loathe to offend them. He has a dependence upon some and it is dangerous crossing them—in such cases he needs a great deal of help from Christ to strengthen his love and his faith so that he may be bold to do his duty. When Jonah was sent to cry against Ninevah because of their wickedness, his fear mastered him so that he fled to Tarshish (Jonah 1:2–3). He was terrified to think what usage he should meet with, and to avoid the anger of men he exposed himself to the anger of God. Faithfulness may expose them to great sorrows, the fear of which sometimes makes them to be unfaithful. Paul begs prayers on that account. Ephesians 6:19–20: "And for me, that I may open my mouth boldly, to make known the mystery of the gospel, for which I am an ambassador in bonds, that therein I may speak boldly, as I ought to speak."

ANSWER 3. To protect their persons. In times of persecution ministers are more exposed than other men; they are looked on as the head of their party, and the principal spite is against them. Jezebel cut off the prophets of the Lord, so the papists have a particular malice against them. About fifty years ago, two thousand ministers were silenced in England in one day, and many of them were exposed to many wrongs and injuries and needed help from God for their deliverance. Paul was delivered through the presence of God. 2 Timothy 4:17: "The Lord stood with me, and strengthened me, and I was delivered out of the mouth of the lion." Christ promised to deliver Paul. Acts 26:17: "Delivering thee from the people and from the Gentiles to whom I send thee." And so He did many times. If God had not delivered him, he would not have continued in his work as he did, but would have fallen a sacrifice to the rage of his enemies many years before he did. Acts 26:22: "Having obtained help of God I continue unto this day."

ANSWER 4. To succeed in their labors. They need to

be prospered in their labors that there may be a reformation wrought in the land, that those corrupt practices which bring down the judgment of God may be put away. And in order to this they need the help of God. It is God's work to prepare men to reform. 2 Chronicles 29:36: "And Hezekiah rejoiced and all the people, that God had prepared the people, for the thing was done suddenly."

There is need of divine help so that the labors of ministers may be prosperous for the comforting of disconsolate saints. Sometimes they are like Rachel, refusing to be comforted.

There is need of the presence of Christ with ministers for the awakening of sinners and bringing them to Christ. Ministers will preach to no purpose if God does not send His Spirit. Ministers can't open blind eyes, nor raise dead men to life. John 16:7-8: "If I depart I will send the Comforter unto you, and when He is come, He will reprove the world of sin, of righteousness, and of judgment." It is God who adds efficacy to the ordinances. 2 Corinthians 10:4: "The weapons of our warfare are mighty through God to the pulling down of strongholds." It is God who casts out devils. It is Christ's work to build up His Church. It is a divine work to make the arrows of the Word stick in the hearts of men. Ministers may waste their spirits, tire their brains, and weary their bodies to no purpose. If God does not give His blessing to their labors, they may take up that complaint from Isaiah 49:4: "I have laboured in vain, have spent my strength for naught and in vain." Men can remain sottish and unbelieving under the best means. It is God who takes away the heart of stone and gives a heart of flesh (Ezekiel 11:19). Ministers may take pains and write their sermons, but it is God only who writes the law in the hearts of men (Jeremiah 31:33). It is His voice that raises dead souls (John 5:25). The Word of God is the sword of the Spirit.

QUESTION. How will Christ be present with them? How does He engage His presence? How far may we depend on those words of Christ without straining them? If we consider the qualities of many ministers, we cannot conceive any eminent presence of Christ with them, as many of the priests of old were very bad. Jeremiah 2:8: "The priests said not, 'Where is the Lord,' and they that handle the law know Me not: and the pastors have transgressed against Me." So the scribes and Pharisees were very corrupt. Matthew 23:3: "Do not after their works, for they say and do not." And so it is at this day in many countries, especially with some ministers of the gospel: their practices are such as make many to stumble at the law.

ANSWER 1. Christ will be so present with the gospel ministry that His visible kingdom shall be upheld. If some of them are notoriously defective of their duty, yet by those that are in the ministry His work shall be carried on and His kingdom shall be preserved throughout all generations. The gospel shall be preached, and there shall be those who shall make a profession of the truth. The kingdom of Christ is sometimes in a more flourishing condition, and sometimes it withers; but it shall never be destroyed. Daniel 2:44: "In the days of these kings shall the God of heaven set up a kingdom that shall never be destroyed." Matthew 16:18: "Upon this rock will I build My Church, and the gates of hell shall not prevail against it." God has made a donation of an eternal kingdom to Christ. Psalm 72:17: "His name shall endure forever, it shall continue as long as the sun." How many secure, carnal, and corrupt men are in the ministry who contribute very little to the upholding of His kingdom? Yet there shall be such a presence of Christ with some who are in the ministry that neither persecution nor heresy shall prevail to root out the kingdom of Christ. God will so far prosper the labors of the ministry that the Church shall be immortal. There shall be a succession of those who shall make a profession of the gospel. There shall always be witnesses for Christ, though for a long while they prophesy in sackcloth. Christ shall divide the spoil with the mighty.

ANSWER 2. Christ will be so present with them that all the elect shall be brought in. There are a number whose names are written in the Lamb's book of life; there are a number that God has given to Christ, and God will bless the labors of ministers unto their conversion and their perseverance in holiness. Some preach Christ out of love and some for carnal ends. So it was of old. Philippians 1:15: "Some indeed preach Christ even of envy and strife, and some of good will." But Christ so far blesses the preaching and writing of the ministry that all the elect shall be brought in. In some ages many are converted, and in all ages such as belong unto the election of grace. John 6:37: "All that the Father hath given Me shall come unto Me." Romans 11:7: "The election hath obtained." Romans 8:30: "Whom He did predestinate, them He also called, and whom He called, them He also justified."

Whether the means are greater or less, there shall be such a presence of Christ with them so that all whom God has chosen shall be converted. If any of them live under corrupt and vicious ministers, yet they shall not miscarry; the light that they enjoy shall prevail for their conversion and salvation. Psalm 132:16: "I will clothe her priests with salvation." Christ will not lose any of those that the Father has given Him.

ANSWER 3. Christ will be present with many of them and make them gracious. For the advantage of religion God will prepare many godly men to preach the gospel. The piety of ministers is greatly for the promoting of religion. Piety makes them more studious; piety furnishes them with such experience as greatly helps them in their work; piety makes them more faithful to the souls of men; and the sense that people have of their piety causes them to lay the more weight on their words, and causes the Word to fall with more authority on them. God fits men for the ministry. So God fitted Paul: He had chosen him to preach the gospel and converted him in a wonderful manner. Galatians 1:15–16: "It pleased God, who separated me from my mother's womb, and called me by His grace, to reveal His Son in me." God promised of old to raise up a faithful priest (1 Samuel 2:35). And sometimes especially there shall be a great number of faithful preachers. Jeremiah 3:15: "I will give them pastors after Mine own heart, that shall feed them with knowledge and understanding." Christ advises us to pray that it may be so. Matthew 9:38: "Pray ye the Lord of the harvest, that He would send forth laborers into His harvest."

And He does at times eminently answer such prayers. So He did at the time of the casting off of popery, which Revelations 14:6 has reference unto: "I saw another angel fly in the midst of heaven, having the everlasting gospel to preach to them that dwell on the earth." God raised up Luther, Melanchthon, Zwingli, and Calvin, along with many others, who did great service to the Church of God. God converts some men and then makes them ministers. So He did with Paul. He made him faithful, and so put him into the ministry (1 Timothy 1:12). And He puts some men into the ministry and then converts them. They are qualified with gifts and learning before, and after they are entered into the work God qualifies them with grace. Acts 6:7: "A great company of the priests were obedient unto the faith."

ANSWER 4. Christ will be graciously present with those who are faithful. It is a great commendation of a minister to be a faithful man. Colossians 1:7: "Epaphras is for you a faithful minister of Christ." Such men shall have the gracious presence of God. He will own them in their work, though it may be in different degrees. God doesn't give the same light to one faithful man that He does to another. Some godly men are left to great mistakes. Godliness is no security against lesser errors. Neither does He give the like measure of protection to one as to another. He appears more eminently for the preservation of one, and the vindication of one, than of another. He eminently vindicated Moses as a reward of his faithfulness. Numbers 12:7: "My servant Moses is not so, who is faithful in all My house." So He does more eminently succeed the labors of one than of another. Some have more abundant success, while some men take abundance of pains and there appears little profit. Others have great occasion to rejoice that they have not run in vain. Paul had great success. Romans 15:29: "I am sure that when I come unto you, I shall come in the fullness of the blessing of the gospel of Christ."

USE 1. This is ground of encouragement to people in praying for the presence of God with their ministers. The minister should pray for the people, and the people should pray for their ministers—for their own ministers and for the ministers of the land—yea, and for the ministers of the Christian world. Moses prays for the ministers. Deuteronomy 33:8: "And of Levi he said, 'Let Thy thummim, and Thy urim be with the Holy One.' " Verse 11: "Bless, Lord, his substance, and accept the work of his hands." David did so in Psalm 132:9: "Let Thy priests be clothed with righteousness." There is ground of encouragement in that Christ has promised His presence with them. This promise may make you bold and free in praying for them; you may conclude that it is acceptable to God so to do. You may gather from this promise that you are welcome to pray for them, that it is a thing suitable to the heart of God, and that there is great hope that God will accept such prayers. Indeed, God does not oblige Himself as to the degree of this mercy, but you have no reason to be discouraged. He allows you to put Him in mind of His promise, and to beg Him that He would remember His Word and fulfill it graciously. You should look on this mercy as a mercy that God delights to bestow, and so come boldly to the throne of grace for it.

But God is not likely to bless ministers' prayers:

1. When people pray for them for form's sake. Many people have a custom when they make their prayers to say something in a cursory way for their ministers; but it is not upon their heart that God would be with them.

We have many people who are violently carrying on worldly designs, who are panting after the dust of the earth, who make light of the gospel, and go one to his farm and another to his merchandise. These men are but formal in their prayers for spiritual blessings. They spend, it may be, the greatest part of their time in prayer about spiritual blessings, but their hearts don't go with their words. So they pray for their ministers, but it is only, of course, because it is their manner; their hearts are not much in it that the labors of their ministers be blessed, either to others or to themselves. When the words are out of their mouths they have done with it; they think no more on it; they don't look after their prayers to see what answer God gives them. If they are not heard they don't trouble themselves; their hearts are not on the prosperity of religion; there is much of Gallio's spirit in them. They care not for those matters (Acts 18:17).

2. When people pray under the prevailings of discouragement. Some persons pray that God would bless their ministers. Conscience of duty makes them do it, and they can't satisfy their own hearts to neglect it; but they think it is not worth the while to insist upon it, for there is very little hope of obtaining any great matter, for things are growing worse and worse in the country. We grow more and more proud, worldly, and intemperate, and there seems to be a blast upon ordinances; people hold fast deceit and refuse to return to God. We seem to be like the people of Judah to whom God sent the prophets, rising early and sending them, but they would not hear. They conclude that the country will degenerate more and more; they say temptations increase and are greatly multiplied; a spirit of rudeness

and profaneness abounds in the land; and they are
ready to say that God seems to have little regard to
prayers of this nature. God has forgotten us, and our
bones are dried" (Ezekiel 37:11) They look so dark that
they are out of hope of obtaining any great matter; they
think the country will grow into a wicked country; they
grow out of heart, and don't seek earnestly that it may
be otherwise.

3. When men pray presumptuously for them. Some
err on this hand, either from a misunderstanding of
the promises, as if God were so bound to bless the
labors of His ministers, that He had not left Himself at
liberty, as certainly He sometimes does in judgment.
Isaiah 6:9: "Go tell this people, 'Hear ye indeed but understand not, and see ye indeed but perceive not'; make
the heart of this people fat, and make their ears heavy,
and shut their eyes, lest they see with their eyes and
hear with their ears, and understand with their hearts,
and convert and be healed." Some presume from
ignorance of the state of the country. They think that
most of the professors of the country are godly men;
they are not sensible that there are many foolish virgins, that many who have a name that they live are
really dead. Many have not the wedding garment; a little appearance passes with them for holiness; they are
somewhat startled to consider that there are so many
judgments in the land, but it seems to them that the
country is full of good people, and that there is a great
number of converted men and women in the land. So
they presume that ministers still will have a great deal
of success, and that religion will flourish in the land.
Some presume upon their prayers, as if they merited to
be heard; as if their earnest prayers must engage God,

and it would not be fair for God to deny them—whereas
if their prayers are answered it is from free grace.

USE 2. Faithful ministers ought to take encouragement that they shall have Christ's presence. Ministers
are in danger of being discouraged. Their work is heavy
and attended with a great deal of difficulty, and their
spirits are ready to faint sometimes under a sense of
their own weakness, want of understanding, and grace
for their work. Sometimes it is upon experience of un-
successfulness; they have taken a great deal of pains,
and little comes of it. Sins that they reprove are not reformed; sinners are not converted; many remain senseless and hard-hearted, as if no means had been used
with them. But their hearts should not sink under their
burden. 2 Corinthians 4:1: "Seeing we have this ministry, as we have received mercy, we faint not." Christ
Jesus can assist them in their work, and furnish them
to do their work acceptably. He can make their work
prosperous. He can make their work powerful, though
men are very blind and dead, and have strong inclinations to continue in a course of sin. Christ has
promised His presence. He does not say that He will be
as much with one as with another, or in what degree
He will be present, but He promises His presence—this
should encourage them.

This shows that Christ is sensible that they need His
presence. When Christ says, "I will be with you," He
speaks it in pity and compassion. He takes notice that
their work is hard, and they are likely to meet with
many difficulties. He is sensible that their work will be
too hard for them if He should leave them alone. He
has no expectation that the work will prosper unless He

is present with them. He knows and takes notice of
their inabilities, that, let them study never so much,
and be exceedingly careful in their preparations, and
earnest and hearty in their delivery of their sermons, let
them use the most proper arguments, follow them
never so fully, confirm what they say by clear testimony
from the Word of God, and pursue the design without
weariness, yet they will not be able to convince or convert men. They can neither reform the place, nor prevail with men to comply with the terms and the gospel,
unless He is present with them. He has no dependence
upon their abilities to make the gospel efficacious. He
is sensible that it would be a fruitless thing to send
them. He may as well send them to remove mountains
as to persuade men to fall in with the way of salvation
unless He is with them. Christ is so well acquainted
with the blindness and hardness of men's hearts that it
will signify nothing to send them unless He is with
them; therefore He promises divine help. John 16:7–8:
"The Comforter shall come and convince the world."

2. He would have them encourage themselves in
hope of His presence. The very design of these words is
to comfort and encourage their hearts. He speaks these
words to support them so that they may go cheerfully
about their work. He would have them set this promise
against the difficulties of their work. He speaks these
words to answer their temptations and the objections
that might arise in their hearts. If He says He will be
with them, He will not call it presumption for them to
hope for His presence; but He will be angry with them
if they do not. Not to be encouraged is to neglect the
proper use of these words. These words, "I will be with
you," are a good foundation for them to pray in faith

for it.

3. Christ is under bonds to grant His presence to the ministry. This promise is absolute to the ministry. I can't say that Christ is absolutely bound to make every minister an instrument of the conversion of souls. A minister may die quickly, or a minister may prove to be a very corrupt man; or, if God should not make a minister an instrument to convert souls, yet He may make him very successful as to establishing and comforting saints, to reform the place, or to clear up some divine truths that were not acknowledged. But this promise, that Christ will be with the ministers, and make use of them for the conversion of souls, is absolute to the ministry. There is no condition expressed, neither is there any to be understood, for it is by the service of the ministry that He intends to carry on His work and build up His church in all generations. Ephesians 4:11–12: "He gave some apostles, some prophets, some evangelists, some pastors, some teachers, for the perfecting of the saints, for the work of the ministry, for the edifying of the body of Christ." And He has elect ones to be brought in all ages. There shall be a succession of godly ones to the end of the world. Psalm 72:17: "His name shall endure forever, it shall continue as long as the sun, men shall be blessed in Him." The success of the ministry is held forth in that parable in Matthew 22:10: "Those servants went out into the highways and gathered together as many as they found, both good and bad, and the wedding was furnished with guests."

4. Add this likewise, that He has made good this word many times eminently. The apostles had great success in one country and another. Acts 14:1: "They so spake that a great multitude both of the Jews and of the

Greeks believed." In Acts 19:20 it is said, "So mightily grew the word of God and prevailed." This success in the primitive times is represented in Revelation 6:2: "Behold a white horse, and he that sat on him had a bow, and a crown was given to him, and he went forth conquering and to conquer." There were many in those days who suffered martyrdom. Revelation 12:11: "They loved not their lives unto the death." So in succeeding ages, when they broke off from popery, many were converted by the ministry and sealed the truth with their blood. In our days several ministers have had eminent success, and God has given a great blessing to their labors. Many of them have given great evidence of their real conversion by their holy lives and the great comfort which they had in a dying day. Many ministers may say by experience what is said in 2 Corinthians 10:4–5: "The weapons of our warfare are not carnal, but mighty through God to the pulling down of strongholds, casting down imaginations, and every high thing that exalteth itself against the knowledge of God, and bringing into captivity every thought to the obedience of Christ."

USE 3. Ministers should do what they can that they may have the presence of Christ with them. It is true that Christ acts somewhat arbitrarily in this matter, yet there are rules to be attended that you may engage the presence of Christ with you. It is well worth the while to take care in this matter. It is a great comfort and encouragement to a minister to see the presence of Christ with his labors. It is a smile upon him. Though it is no certain sign of sincerity, yet therein God smiles on him; it is an honor to him. When God sets His seal to his ministry, God owns him in his work. 1 Corinthians

9:2: "The seal of my apostleship are ye in the Lord." When God is present with his labors He makes him a blessing, which was part of the happiness of Abraham. God told him, "I will bless thee and thou shalt be a blessing" (Genesis 12:2). Dr. Williams, Bishop of Lincoln, in his old age, expressed himself in this manner: he had held many honorable offices, but if he knew that he had been an instrument to convert one soul to God, it would be more comfort to him than all the offices that he had sustained. To be useless is a reproach, to be an instrument to do hurt is a curse, but to be an instrument of good is a great honor. So, then:

Be of an unblamable conversation. The holy carriages of ministers have a natural tendency to beget a regard in the hearts of hearers. Holy carriages command respect and prepare men to receive advice. They are more ready to believe men of good conversation than men of bad conversation. Holy carriages in preachers take prejudices off from the spirits of hearers. It seems to men that such ministers urge rules from conscience and compassion. But an unholy conversation diminishes men's authority, their words don't sink into the hearts of their hearers, they don't look upon their advice as flowing from a gracious spirit, but from some lower principles. But men of holy conversation have a room in the hearts of others. Besides, this is a way to engage the presence of Christ. Evil carriages are abominable to Christ, but holy carriages are acceptable to Christ. Men who walk holily put honor upon Him, and He will honor those who honor Him (1 Samuel 2:30). When men carry holily, God delights to succeed their labors. Malachi 2:6: "He walked with Me in peace and equity, and did turn many away from iniquity." But when men carry corruptly He many times casts contempt on them, and their ministry is not blessed. Malachi 2:8–9: " 'But ye are departed out of the way; ye have caused many to stumble at the law; ye have corrupted the covenant of Levi,' saith the Lord of hosts. 'Therefore have I also made you contemptible and base before all the people; according as ye have not kept My ways, but have been partial in the law.' " An unholy conversation brings a blast upon their labors. The prosperity of religion doesn't depend on the labors of men who do not honor it. Their words will not prevail without their practice. They must preach in their conversation on weekdays as well as in the pulpit on the Sabbath.

Insist on those things that men stand in special need of. All Scripture is profitable, but the great design of the Scripture and the ministry is to convert men to God. Acts 26:18: "To open their blind eyes, to turn them from darkness to light, and from the power of Satan unto God." Some ministers speak a great deal to saints to comfort and encourage them; and, alas, there are but a few of them in many congregations. The most of the people are in a perishing condition, and there is ten times more need that men be awakened and terrified. Ministers should imitate Paul. 2 Corinthians 5:11: "Knowing the terror of the Lord, we persuade men." Christ Jesus was often putting men in mind of hell and the day of judgment in the time of His ministry. It is not a little hint now and then that will make them work out their salvation with fear and trembling. Many men are in a fast sleep, and whispering will not awaken them; the threatenings of God need to ring in their ears; they are so atheistic and devoted to the world that it is well if thunder and lightning will scare them. They are so hardened that talking moderately to them, as Eli did to his sons, makes no more impression on them than on the seats of the meeting house. The rule is (Ezekiel 6:11), "Thus saith the Lord God, 'Smite with thy hand, and stamp with thy foot, and say, "Alas," for all the abominations of the house of Israel, for they shall fall by the sword, and by the famine, and by the pestilence.' "

Preach in such a manner as is most proper to take with the conscience. God's way is to bless suitable means. He doesn't bless healing plasters to eat away proud flesh. He doesn't bless cordials to take away stubborn humors. If ministers design to convert men, they need to speak piercing words. Ecclesiastes 12:11: "The words of the wise are as goads and as nails, fastened by the Master of assemblies." Some ministers affect rhetorical strains of speech, as if they were making an oration in the schools; this may tickle the fancies of men, and scratch itching ears; but we have men's consciences to deal with. Men need to be frightened and not to be pleased. 1 Corinthians 2:4: "My speech and my preaching was not with enticing words of man's wisdom; but in demonstration of the Spirit and of power." We are not sent into the pulpit to show our wit and eloquence, but to set the consciences of men on fire; not to nourish the vain humors of people, but to lance and wound the consciences of men. "The Word is sharper than a two-edged sword, dividing soul and spirit, joints and marrow, discovering the thoughts and intents of the heart" (Hebrews 4:12). And we should use it for that end. The Word is as a hammer, and we should use it to break the rocky hearts of men.

Be much in prayer for the presence of Christ. Christ has made a promise, but He expects that we should sue it out. Ezekiel 36:37: "Yet will I be inquired of by the house of Israel to do it for them." We should turn promises into petitions. One end of promises is to help us to pray in faith, and this is a way to engage Christ more eminently to fulfill the promise. When we pray for the presence of Christ, we acknowledge our own insufficiency, and that we have need of the presence of Christ; that we can neither do our work nor obtain success without Him. When we pray for His presence, we acknowledge that we are unworthy of it; that we cannot challenge it as due, but depend on His grace to make it good to us; that we must have it in a way of free gift. When we pray for it, we acknowledge His sufficiency to help us; that if we have His presence, that will be enough, that then we may go cheerfully on in our work. When we pray for it, we show that we lay weight upon His promise, and it is a sign that if He does grant His presence we shall give Him the glory and ascribe our success to Him. Therefore we had need be much in prayer for this, that God's urim and thumim may with us. This is our encouragement, that He has said that He will clothe His priests with salvation (Psalm 132:16), and, as in the text, that He will be with His ministers to the end of the world.

The Duty of Gospel Ministers to Preserve a People from Corruption

(A sermon preached at Brookfield October 16, 1717,
being the day wherein the church was gathered
and Mr. Thomas Cheny was ordained pastor)

"Ye are the salt of the earth." Matthew 5:13

Christ Jesus, having been baptized and, after that, tempted of Satan for forty days, does in a more eminent manner enter into the execution of His prophetic office, and preaches His "Sermon On The Mount," contained in this and the following two chapters of Matthew. He begins His sermon by teaching them who are the "blessed" men, and then, in this verse and the next, teaches His disciples what is their office, and the work which they are to do as His ministers.

First, He tells them that they are "the salt of the earth." It may be inquired who He speaks to. Some think that it is spoken of professed Christians. But that does not seem proper, for then when countries come to be christianized there would be no difference between the salt and those who are salted. Christ knew that whole nations would entertain the Christian religion, and who then would they be salt unto? But I judge that He intends the apostles, and it may be the seventy disciples, if they were present at that time. Though they were not yet called to their office, yet Christ designed them to it.

We find a distinction in verse 1 between His auditors and His disciples: "Seeing the multitudes, He went up into a mountain, and when He was seated His disciples came unto Him." Again we may inquire why Christ compares them to salt.

Salt has many useful qualities. It has medicinal virtues in it, applied outwardly or inwardly; but it has two properties especially: one is that it savors meats and gives a grateful relish to them, making them more acceptable to the stomach, taking away their crudeness, and is therefore a help to digestion. Job 6:6: "Can that which is unsavory be taken without salt?" The other is that it preserves things from corruption and putrefaction. Flesh and some other meats are liable in a little time to corrupt and spoil; but salt has virtue to preserve them, and it is in this respect that the apostles are compared to salt. He does not speak of what they were *de facto,* but of what they were *de jure,* what they were by their office to be.

Again, it may be inquired who would have the benefit. The answer would be the earth, or the land where they dwell. By earth you are to understand the inhabitants of the earth. This is amplified by their uncurableness if they lose their savor. Not but that a minister may be recovered if he loses his savor, but if the ministry should lose its savor, there is none to recover them. And he also loses his savor if by his unprofitableness he grows corrupt and unsavory. Those ministers are unserviceable and deserve to be rejected. "It is good for nothing but to be cast out and trodden under foot of men."

DOCTRINE. The ministers of the gospel are by their office to preserve the people from corruption.
It is a great misery to a people to be corrupted, to be like putrified and rotten meat. They will be an affliction and enemies one to another, and exposed unto the judgments of God. But the ministers of the gospel are means to preserve them from corruption. Magistrates, in their place, have their influence on them to preserve them from corruption; but especially ministers are useful that way. In such nations where there is no gospel ministry, people are very corrupt. If by the light of nature and the severity of rulers they are preserved from grosser iniquities, yet they are always very corrupt. But the faithful services of gospel ministers is a special help to preserve from corruptions. A gospel ministry is looked upon by some persons as a heavy charge; they groan under the burden of it. But men have little reason to think much of the charge considering the benefit that they are to a people, as they are means to prevent the growing of corruption. Ministers need to be careful that they fulfill their ministry, for their work is not only of great concern to themselves, but also to multitudes of others by keeping the country from corruption.
1. Consider that people are very prone to grow corrupt. As the bodies of men, if they are not duly looked after, will grow corrupt, so will the souls of men. A professing people are in great danger, many of them are in their natural condition, and godly men who are among them are but in part sanctified. There are a great many young ones growing up among them who are born in sin and an abundance of temptations; and there is a great deal of danger that in a little time they will be

corrupted. As buildings are subject to decay and fields to be tainted, so people are subject to being corrupted. Isaiah 1:21: "How is the faithful city become an harlot!"

(1) In respect of the principles of religion. The Church of God is called "the pillar and ground of truth" (1 Timothy 3:15). And if they don't hold fast the form of wholesome words they will quickly run to ruin. The practice of religion depends upon the principles: if they lose the knowledge of the truth they can't make due improvement of it. Blindness is a corruption and it leads to corrupt practices.

They are in danger of corruption by ignorance. A knowing people may in time become an ignorant people. The people of Greece were some of the most learned people in the world in former generations. Corinth and Athens were called the two eyes of the world; but since that they have become very ignorant. Darkness many times succeeds where there was a great deal of light. If the present generation is comprised of knowing men, in a few years many of them may die and the young generation, if they do not have suitable means of instruction, will be very ignorant. Though they grow to years of understanding, they may be ignorant of the principles of religion. Parents may bequeath their estates to them, but they can't bequeath their knowledge to them. If their teachers are blind and ignorant, as the complaint is in Isaiah 56:10, it is no wonder if the people are ignorant. The people of Israel grew in continuance of time a very ignorant people. Hosea 4:1: "There is no knowledge of God in the land." If a people is a knowing people, yet by the change of a generation they may be children in understanding.

They are in danger of corruption by errors. Men have a

great deal of carnal reason, and so are in danger of growing erroneous. There are a great many temptations from without to errors; there are many false doctrines published in the world. Men have mightily corrupted the doctrine of the Christian religion. There have been heretical teachers who have broached dangerous errors. 2 Peter 2:1: "There shall be false teachers among you, who shall privily bring in damnable heresies." And Satan is busy to blind the minds of men. 2 Corinthians 4:4:" The god of this world has blinded their minds."

And there are many temptations in men's own hearts to seduce them. Carnal men don't love evangelical truths, and the pride of their hearts exposes them. They are unwilling to acknowledge such truths as they cannot comprehend. The lusts of men's hearts incline them to receive heretical doctrines. 2 Timothy 3:6: "They lead captive silly women laden with sins, led away with divers lusts." Many errors have mightily prevailed in the world. "The smoke that has come out of the bottomless pit has darkened the air" (Revelation 9:2). Arianism did so for awhile, then Pelagianism, popery, and Arminianism—many countries are corrupted.

(2) In respect of practice. Fallen men are great enemies to the power of godliness and in great danger of carrying themselves corruptly. It is difficult to make a professing people grow better, but they easily grow worse. It is natural to those who have chronic diseases to grow worse and worse. People who are in a declining way are in great danger to decline more and more. Jeremiah 16:12: "Ye have done worse than your fathers." Land that begins to be tainted is liable to be tainted more and more.

By formality. Where the worship of God is set up, men don't readily lose the form; but it is a frequent thing to lose the *power* of godliness. It is an easy thing to carry on praying, to attend public worship, and to attend duties of religion on the Sabbath. This may be done, though their hearts are violently set against the Word and they are under great prevailings of evil affections; but it is very cross to nature to mortify corruptions and to exercise themselves in self-denial, to give their hearts to God, and to be rejoicing in the righteousness of Christ. Many times people who retain the name of living lose the life of religion (Revelation 3:1). People are wont to grow lukewarm (Revelation 3:16). The spirit of religion decays by degrees.

By vices. Evil practices frequently gain ground among them. The lusts of men's hearts hurry them into bold transgressions. There are bad examples and small means of restraints, and so evil practices get headway. Many times people grow knavish and injurious one to another; they have their ways of deceit and oppression that mightily prevail. Jeremiah 6:6: "She is wholly oppression in the midst of her."

Sometimes they fall into ways of drunkenness and lie at the tavern; they are pouring in strong drink, and they can't work without it, nor play without it, nor make bargains without it. They love bottles of wine, fall into ways of wantonness and rudeness. Sin abounds in all professing countries.

2. Consider how ministers are to preserve a people from corruption.

(1) They are to do it by their preaching. Ministers are God's messengers or ambassadors, sent to publish the gospel. Mark 16:15: "Preach the gospel to every

creature," i.e., every human creature. This is the principal part of their work. 1 Corinthians 1:17: "Christ sent me not to baptize, but to preach the gospel." Therefore they are called "preachers." 1 Timothy 2:7: "I am ordained a preacher." Other services are to be done occasionally, but this is the constant service that they must addict themselves unto. 2 Timothy 4:2: "Preach the word, be instant in season, out of season."

And it is upon this account especially that double honor is due unto them. 1 Timothy 5:17: "Let the elders that rule well be counted worthy of a double honor, especially they that labor in the word and doctrine." The Word of God duly preached is the special means to advance the work of sanctification. John 17:17: "Sanctify them by Thy truth, Thy Word is that truth."

By instructing them in the principles of religion and the rules of God's Word. The light of nature teaches men some things concerning God and His attributes, and it teaches them the difference concerning many things that are morally good and evil; but this light shines but dimly, and the characters that are written in the heart are much blurred and obliterated. So men have need to have those things clearly indicated. But the way of salvation by Christ is a thing of pure revelation. Natural reason is utterly silent about it. The gospel is called "the wisdom of God" in 1 Corinthians 2:7. The work of the minister is to feed men with the "sincere milk of the Word," and to feed the sheep and the lambs (John 21:15–16). It is not enough that men are able to say their catechism by rote, but the minister must labor in it that they may have a confirmed knowledge of the truth, that they may have a clear, distinct, and explicit understanding of the doctrines of religion. They must take pains to make them understand. Hebrews 5:12: "Ye need that one teach you again the first principles of the oracles of God."

(2) They are to do it by solemn warnings. That was Paul's practice. Acts 20:31: "I ceased not to warn every one of you night and day with tears." That is the duty of the watchman (Ezekiel 33:8). There is great danger many times of public calamities because of the abounding of sin among them. The watchman must warn them and reprove them. Isaiah 58:1: "Cry aloud, spare not, lift up thy voice like a trumpet, show My people their transgression, and the house of Israel their sin." Godly men are in danger of provoking God and bringing sorrow upon themselves—and the minister must warn them. Many lie in a natural condition, and in danger of damnation; they need to be turned (Mark 16:16). Some are of an unruly and ungoverned conversation. If they continue so, their end will be destruction—these must be warned (1 Thessalonians 5:14). Many men who are in a dangerous way are severe and bold, and the minister must set the terrors of God before them, putting them in mind of the jealousy of God and the terribleness of His indignation. There are many Scriptures wherein God speaks terribly to ungodly men; and ministers should make those Scriptures ring in their ears and be with utmost solemnity telling them of their danger. Philippians 3:18–19: "Many walk of whom I have told you often, and now tell you weeping, that they are enemies of the cross of Christ, whose end is destruction."

(3) They are to do it by suitable encouragement. Awakened sinners are in danger, though seldom of despairing, yet of being discouraged. That will be a great

wrong to them, and ministers must be careful to encourage them. God puts such words into their mouths
(Isaiah 55:6–8). Matthew 11:28: "Come unto Me, all ye
that are weary and heavy laden." Some are in danger of
being discouraged from doing their duty, from fear of
want, from fear of the anger of man, for fear of reproach. But there are many promises in the Word of
God to strengthen men's hearts in such cases. Galatians 6:9: "Let us not be weary in well doing, for in due
season we shall reap if we faint not." Some are ready to
sink in their spirits because of their afflictions, their
sins, their temptations, and their dangers. It is very fit
that such should be encouraged. 1 Thessalonians 5:14:
"Comfort the feeble-minded, support the weak."

(4) Ministers should preserve a people from corruption by good government. God has given power of
ruling to ministers. Hebrews 13:17: "Obey them that
rule you and submit to them." He has given a power of
binding and loosing. Matthew 16:19: "What thou shalt
bind on earth shall be bound in heaven." And He ap-
points that they rule well (1 Timothy 5:17). Ministers
have a coercive power to execute censures on those who
are obstinate. Ministers must have a tender and com-
passionate spirit, but, when men are sturdy and rebellious, severity is compassion. Executing ecclesiastical
censures is "a terror to evildoers." This is a proper
means so that their "spirits may be saved in the day of
the Lord Jesus" (1 Corinthians 5:5). Though private revenge is utterly forbidden, yet they are to revenge disobedience. 2 Corinthians 10:6: "Having in a readiness
to revenge all disobedience." This is the way to purge
out the old leaven, to bring men to repentance, and to
put a stop to growing iniquities so that the land is

not defiled.

(5) Ministers should preserve a people from corruption by being good examples. Ministers must be examples to the people in all virtuous carriages. When ministers teach men their duty, they must be obedient whether the minister practices so or not. Matthew 23:3: "Whatsoever they bid you observe, that observe and do; but do not yet after their works, for they say and do not." But ministers need to give good examples. 1 Timothy 4:12: "Be thou an example of the believers in word, in conversation, in charity, in spirit, in faith, in purity." If they give a good example their words will sink more into the hearts of men. But if they addict themselves to any vice, men will despise them and their counsels and warnings; they will judge that they don't believe themselves what they say; they will nauseate their preaching. It would be very unpleasant to hear a Pharisee make a grave harangue against hypocrisy, to hear a Judas declaim against stealing. If ministers are not of good conversation, people will count their preaching to be art and dissimilation; it will render them contemptible in the eyes of the people (Malachi 2:8–9). Men could hardly be patient to hear a drunkard speak in the commendation of temperance or a wanton man enlarge in the commendation of chastity.

USE 1. A faithful ministry in a land is a great blessing. If God gives a people a good crop, if He gives peace and health, they count it as having received great blessings. And yet they take little notice of the mercy of God in giving a faithful ministry unto them; but God reckons this a great mercy. Jeremiah 3:15: "I will give them pastors after Mine own heart, that shall feed them with knowledge and understanding." Amos 2:11: "I raised up some of your sons for prophets." They are great blessings on this account: they are the salt of the land. If men's provisions should putrify for lack of salt it would be a great calamity; but if the people of the land should grow corrupt for lack of a faithful ministry, that would be a far greater calamity. When they are faithful they are a means to prevent corruption. Malachi 2:6: "He walked with Me in peace and equity, and did turn many away from iniquity." That is great service:

1. For if they should be corrupt, they would be a great affliction one to another. When people carry orderly and holily they will be a great comfort one to another. They will make their conversation and society pleasant and profitable, and they will dwell together in unity. Religion teaches men to love one another, but when they are corrupt they will be as thorns in one another's sides. Micah 7:4: "The best of them is a briar, the most upright is sharper than a thornhedge." They will be reproaching and backbiting one another, blasting the names of one another. Children will carry badly to parents, and parents to their children. They will be injurious to one another's estates, cheating, oppressing, stealing; they will be quarrelling and fighting; they will be debauching one another; they will corrupt men's daughters and wives too; they will be plagues one to another.

2. Then their prosperity will do them hurt. If God bestows plenty and success on them, they will be taken with it and, it may be, keep days of thanksgiving; but they had better be without their prosperity. Their blessings will become curses; their meat will be their portion; their prosperity will make them more secure and

hard-hearted. They will flatter themselves and take the more liberty to be wicked; they will put false constructions on the providence of God, take occasion to flatter themselves, take the more liberty to carry loosely; they will take a liberty to be drunken and live an effeminate life. Deuteronomy 32:15: "But Jeshurun waxed fat and kicked, thou art waxen fat, thou art grown thick, thou art covered with fatness; therefore he forsook God that made him, and lightly esteemed the Rock of his salvation." So they will grow more covetous; their prosperity will be like oil to feed the flame. It would be better for them to have been kept poor and low. Proverbs 1:32: "The prosperity of fools shall destroy them."

3. They will have a great deal of judgment. If they prosper awhile it won't continue, but God will pursue them with the tokens of His anger. When Israel corrupted themselves in the wilderness, the plague came amongst them and many fell; sometimes serpents bit them. When they corrupted themselves in the land of Canaan, God sent the Mesopotamians, Moabites, Midians, Ammorites, and Philistines upon them, and brought them into great distress (Judges 5:8). God is a jealous God and will not let their sins go unrevenged. God has His day of judgment wherein they shall be called to an account; and then they will cry to God and He will not hear. Iniquity is a root that bears gall and wormwood, and their sins will cost them dearly. Job 21:17: "God distributeth sorrows in His anger."

4. Multitudes of them will perish. When religion flourishes among a people, they don't all go to heaven when they die. Many have but a name that they live. There is chaff as well as wheat; there are foolish virgins among the wise. But when it is a corrupt time, few are

converted and the means of grace are much blasted. Men are minding their carnal enjoyments more than heaven. They have great temptations and the temptations have great power. Few of them will find their way to heaven; there will be but a small number of godly men; they will fail much as in Saul's time. Psalm 12:1: "Help, Lord, for the godly man ceaseth, for the faithful fail from among the children of men." They will depend much upon their privileges and outward services, and generally, as they die, they will go to hell. Hell will be stocked with them. An evil generation is a generation of God's wrath. So when Christ was here (Matthew 8:12), "the children of the kingdom shall be cast out into outer darkness, there shall be wailing and gnashing of teeth."

USE 2. People need to be careful that they don't provoke God to give them such a ministry as will be like unsavory salt. Sometimes God leaves a people to such a ministry. Isaiah 56:10: "His watchmen are blind, they are all ignorant, they are all dumb dogs that cannot bark; sleeping, lying down, loving to slumber." Jeremiah 2:8: "The priests said not, 'Where is the Lord?' and they that handle the law knew Me not, and the pastors have transgressed against Me." Zechariah 11:15–16: "The Lord said to me, 'Take unto thee the instruments of a foolish shepherd, for I will raise a shepherd in the land that shall not visit that which is cut off.' "

When God does so it is in a way of punishment. It is a sign that such a people have greatly offended God; this is one way whereby God pours out His displeasure upon a provoking people. And, when He does so, they are likely to grow more and more corrupt. The scribes and Pharisees were such ministers: they were blind guides, and the guide and the people both fell into the ditch. Therefore you should avoid such sins as may bring this judgment. There is often a suitableness between the sin and the punishment. You may bring this judgment:

By barrenness under a fruitful ministry. It is sometimes so that faithful ministers have very little success. They take a great deal of pains, and there is very little effect of it. Men dote upon the world, despise the gospel, don't regard rules, make their hearts like an adamant, and make a derision of the awful threatenings of the Word of God. God, in this case, sometimes takes away their opportunities.

When the people of Judah brought forth only wild grapes, God threatened this judgment (Isaiah 5:6): "I will lay it waste, and it shall not be pruned nor digged, but there shall come up briars and thorns, and I will command the clouds that they rain no rain upon it." When men don't profit by means, it is just with God to take away suitable means. God in anger gives them up to strong delusions, sends them such teachers as shall mislead them and be a snare to them. And so they grow into corrupt principles; they did not like sound doctrine, and they are fitted with such teachers as shall nourish a spirit of security in them. 2 Thessalonians 2:10–12: "Because they received not the love of the truth, God shall send them strong delusion, that they should believe a lie."

By abusing a faithful ministry. Sometimes people cannot endure sound doctrine, and misuse God's prophets. 2 Chronicles 36:16: "They mocked the messengers of God, and despised His word, and misused

His prophets." They give them a great deal of trouble and molestation; they oppose them, contradict them, and weakened their hands in their work. Sometimes they talk against them (Ezekiel 33:31). Sometimes they persecute them. This is a great provocation to God, and He, many times, punishes them by leaving them to a corrupt and carnal ministry that will do them little good, and sometimes to such as will do them a great deal of hurt. Thus God dealt with the people of Israel: they abused the prophets that God had sent unto them and God took vengeance on them by leaving them to false prophets who deluded them and were the occasion of their ruin. Lamentations 2:14: "Thy prophets have seen vain and foolish things."

By counting their ministry a burden. Sometimes a sordid spirit prevails among a people, and they count their ministers as bills of charge. They can lavish away a great deal in a year for the gratification of their pride and voluptuousness, and they can spend freely upon many frivolous occasions, but the support of the worship of God is counted a great burden. God may justly remove faithful teachers in a way of anger for this and leave them to such teachers as shall not profit them. God is angry when they think much to maintain His worship. God gives them wherewith to do it, and He does so that they may do it; and they provoke Him when they think that ill spent which is laid out that way. "If ministers sow unto them spiritual things, it is not a great thing if they reap their carnal things" (1 Corinthians 9:11).

USE 3. Let this be the care of ministers. Ministers must do their office in being the salt of the land. We find great complaint of the Jewish ministers before the Babylonian captivity in Isaiah, Jeremiah, and Ezekiel. And after the captivity we find the same in Ezra, Nehemiah, and Malachi. Ministers must not only be careful that they don't corrupt the land by evil manners and false doctrine, but also that they don't, by their negligence, suffer the people to corrupt themselves.

It is a great fault in ministers when they don't diligently study the mind of God, but spend their time in visits and worldly business. 1 Timothy 4:15: "Meditate upon these things, give thyself wholly to them." It is very blameworthy in them when they preach things that they have not studied. It is a great sin in them when they are afraid to deal faithfully and to bear a testimony against the sins of the land. If the land is corrupted by their default, they will bring down the anger of God upon themselves. If they countenance the sins of the land, if they do not do their duty to prevent the sins of the land, they will make themselves partakers of other men's sins; and it will be a dreadful thing for God to charge the sins of the land on them. Malachi 2:8: "Ye have caused many to stumble at the law."

But if they are serviceable according to their place, to keep the land from being corrupted, God will reward them for it. He will be ready to acknowledge their service. Malachi 2:6: "The law of truth was in his mouth, iniquity was not found in his lips, he walked with Me in peace and equity." And it will be a great honor and comfort to them that they have been instruments of the holiness of the land, when the sons of Levi are purified, the offerings of Judah will be acceptable to God (Malachi 3:3–4).

There are four things that ministers should labor in

to prevent the corruption of the land. They should labor:

1. That there are a good number of people savingly converted. Ministers should labor to convert as many as possible, not only out of a respect to the salvation of their souls, but to prevent the corruption of the land. If men are converted they will lead holy lives. 1 John 3:9: "He that is born of God sinneth not." Men who are converted are not so apt to drink in false doctrine as other men, and they will have a great influence upon the conversation of others; but an unconverted generation will be a corrupt generation (Judges 2:10–11). Converted men will teach their children the ways of God and will discountenance sinful practices. Converted men will be good examples, yea, they will savor divine things, and thereby stir up that light that is in the consciences of others. If men who are converted have power, they will improve it for God.

2. That godly men are kept in a flourishing condition. Converted men may be in a withering condition and are carried away with a worldly spirit; but ministers should be careful to keep them in a thriving way that their souls may be in a prosperous condition, that they may be in a healthy estate, and enjoy much of the presence of God. If godly men are under decay, as sometimes they are (Revelation 2:4 speaks of losing their first love), that will be a damage to the religion of a country. When they flourish, they will walk more exactly according to the rules of the gospel. They will be more zealous for God; they will more strongly resist temptation; they will be more savory, and their discourses will be more edifying. Psalm 45:1 says that their hearts will "recite good matter, and their tongues will

be as the pen of a ready writer." They will be more exemplary, and others will be loathe to grieve them.

3. That the consciences of natural men are kept tender. Ministers must labor to possess men with a deep sense of the jealousy of God and of the terrible judgments that God executes for sin. They should often be setting matter of terror before men, reminding them of eternal punishments, of the awful ways wherein God takes vengeance on impenitent sinners, so that they may be afraid of sin. 2 Corinthians 5:11: "Knowing the terrors of the Lord we persuade men." If their consciences are awakened, they will restrain them from sinful practices and bridle in their corruptions. Matthew 19:20: "All these things I have done from my youth." Their fear will dispose them to lead a religious life, and will make them forbear ways of iniquity. Though desitute of grace, yet they will carry themselves commendably.

4. That they are well principled against the errors and vices of the age. Ignorance exposes a people to corrupt carriages. If men's principles are erroneous they will carry badly, whether they are godly or ungodly (2 Timothy 2:16). If men mistake the rule, conscience will allow them to break it; yea, it will *force* them to break it. But if conscience is duly informed, many natural men will not dare to do against their light. Therefore ministers should be careful to principle the people aright about the nature of true conversion, about true signs of grace, and about moral duties. Many men are carried away with the corrupt practices of the land into pride, injustice, and licensiousness because they think they are lawful. If they were well taught they would reform. The Word of God would be like fire in

them: they would not dare to do such things as now they do. When any ill practice prevails, the minister should do as John did (Matthew 14:4): "John said to him, 'It is not lawful for thee to have her.' "